The Paris Diary of Ned Rorem

The Paris Diary of Ned Rorem

WITH A PORTRAIT OF THE DIARIST BY ROBERT PHELPS

GEORGE BRAZILLER NEW YORK

CONTENTS

ix

A PORTRAIT OF THE DIARIST

*Je n'entre pas en ligne de compte que les
oeuvres plaisent ou déplaisent. Elles
doivent "être."* —JEAN COCTEAU

*. . . and there are always those to whom
all self-revelation is contemptible.*
—F. SCOTT FITZGERALD

Here in lonesome, wistful, Puritan America, we are shy about
diaries. We have a few good ones—Alice James's, for instance—
but we make little of them. The ones we tend to read are im-
ports (other people's indiscretions)—Nijinsky's, Virginia
Woolf's, Katherine Mansfield's, Gide's—and we assure ourselves
that we are trespassing only because the diarist is important for
some prior achievement. His book is not an end in itself, never;
and even so, it is only when the text is unintimate and general-
ized, as in the case of Dag Hammarskjöld's, that we read without
guilt.

At the same time, the *idea* of diaries has haunted us. From
almost the beginning, and in our best writers, we can trace a
literary ideal which, whatever you call it, would look and read
like a diary if it were incarnated. Listen to Poe:

> If any ambitious man have a fancy to revolutionize, at
> one effort, the universal world of human thought, human

opinion, and human sentiment, the opportunity is his own
—the road to immortal renown lies straight, open, unen-
cumbered before him. All that he has to do is write and
publish a very little book. Its title should be simple—a
few plain words—"My Heart Laid Bare." But—this little
book must be *true to its title.* No man dare write it. No
man *could* write it, even if he dared. The paper would
shrivel and blaze at every touch of the fiery pen.

Or Thoreau:

I desire to speak somewhere without bounds, like a man
in a waking moment to men in their waking moments.

Or Emerson:

These novels will give way, by and by, to diaries or auto-
biographies—captivating books, if only a man knew how
to choose among what he calls his experiences that which
is really his experience, and how to record truth truly.

Listen to Walt Whitman:

No man can understand any greatness or goodness but his
own, or the indication of his own. . .

Or Howells (writing to Mark Twain):

Even you won't tell the black heart's truth. The man who
could do it would be famed to the last day the sun shone
upon.

Or even Henry James (writing to a young poet):

I am also envious—envious of the lyric mood, the lyric
leak. You can say the egotistical thing—*I never!*

And then think of all those maverick books that keep turning up in American literature, and which sound, more than anything else, like audacious asides to the audience—the novelist or poet appropriating a tone and a form which his official, public art does not quite allow: *Eureka, The Enormous Room, The Crack-Up, Death in the Afternoon* (or the late, as-yet-uncollected memoir called *The Dangerous Summer*), *The American Scene, The Tropic of Cancer, Let Us Now Praise Famous Men, Images of Truth, Life on the Mississippi. . .* It is as though the whole tradition of American writing, underneath its acquiescence to the proprieties of the novel, the short story, the poem, the autobiography, were yearning to give us some less indirect form of the writer's vision and presence—something closer to himself.

I do not mean to sound dogmatic. I have no theory to advance. I simply sense, in much contemporary writing, an instinct (unconscious in some writers, very self-conscious, even precious, in others) to invent, or subpoena, a form in which they can speak more intimately, more precisely, in terms of the authority which their own experience has conferred upon them. And this, in turn, always makes me wonder whether, as readers, we shall ever be able to help these writers to the extent of admitting to the literary canon the convention of the published diary. In other words, I wonder if, sooner or later, we may not allow a man with Poe's ideal to offer us his results directly, in the diary form he himself used, rather than oblige him to translate it all, so to speak, into what we then agree to call a piece of "fiction" (*Herzog*, for instance) and which, inevitably, we later ask biographers to translate back into his original terms. . .

But this can be a dangerous train of speculation. It can make many people impatient and angry. Merely by asking if a diary could not be read for its own sake—as a novel is—I could be charged with unseemly curiosity, or, more gravely, with obscuring the difference between Art and Life, Imagination and

Fact, Making Images and Bearing Witness. "We have art,"
said Nietzsche, "in order that we may not perish from life. . ."
And some of the time, certainly, he is right. We *do* need stories
and songs and plays which seem impersonal, detached from their
creators and uncluttered by a first person. But sometimes we also
need something closer to one man's untidy essence. Oftener
than I'd like to admit, I read a novel or a poem, and am conscious—Nietzsche to the contrary—that we use art chiefly in
order *to hide out* from life. At worst, this stifles me. At best, it
leaves me hungering. Parable, fable, fiction are all fine. I want
them. But whether I can gracefully justify it or not, I also want
diaries, letters, marginalia, table-talk, all the nonofficial literary
forms by which men have also revealed their mystery, disguises,
wishes, feints.

🌰

All of which, I hope not irrelevantly, brings us to the present
book, which amounts to selections from a diary kept between
1951 and 1955 by a young American composer who was living
in France and North Africa. It differs from most diaries I have
read chiefly in that it is better written, more aptly observed, less
fearfully self-guarding. Insofar as there is any plot, it is self-
portraiture, and self-reckoning; but the elements that compose
this particular Self are very exceptional.

At the time he is writing, the author is in his late twenties
(he was born on October 23, 1923) and midwestern by way of
Norwegian ancestors. He is gifted, good-looking, and in the
circles in which he moves, celebrated for both. Besides being a
composer, he is an imaginative social climber, a Quaker (though
he sounds more like a Calvinist at times), an earnest narcissist.
He is also an intellectual, a hero-worshiper, an excessive drinker
of alcohol, and a lover—or more exactly, the sort of sensual man
Montherlant must have had in mind when he said *"le corps fait
trop l'âme pour qu'on doive s'excuser quand on parle de lui."*

At the same time (otherwise he could not have been so good a diarist) he is a born watcher, with a shrewd sense of theater, and rarest of all, the gift of recollection. It is one thing—luck, or connivance—to encounter Poulenc, Alice B. Toklas, Cocteau, Paul Eluard or the Vicomtesse de Noailles; it is another to be able to remember and record something they actually said, or did, or how they looked. Ned Rorem gives us specific *choses vues*, and so among other things his diary becomes a small but valid documentary on Paris in the early Fifties. By the time he arrived, Valéry had already said *"l'Europe est finie,"* and in some sense, perhaps it was. But part of Valéry's own Paris still flourished, and the last of a generation of its ringleaders—Cocteau, Poulenc, Auric—were still calling the tune. There was silliness and phoniness and pretention. There was also cultivation and appetite and enterprise. The arts were not necessarily better understood in Paris. But they did enjoy the prestige accorded elsewhere only to politics and sports and the weather. Moreover, it was not unknown for a great lady to offer a young composer the use of her salon for a concert and to invite a hundred people who had once heard Stravinsky and Ravel play their own music in the same precincts. Other gifted young Americans were living in Paris at the same time—William Styron, James Baldwin, George Plimpton. But they lived among themselves, on the left bank. Ned Rorem lived with the French, in the *16e arrondissement,* and this is an important part of his self-portrait.

But it is his own personality that is principally embodied here, and which, at least for me, has made his diary such resonant and nutritious reading. In the decade since it was written, Ned has become, relatively speaking, well-known, even famous. He has been called "the world's best composer of art songs," and in the past season (1965–66) his first full-length opera, *Miss Julie,* had its New York première. But still, for many of his potential readers, he is probably not famous enough to enable his diary to offer itself as an adjunct to his career, as, say, Leonard Bernstein's might be, or Stravinsky's conversation books are. It must therefore be offered, and read, for its own sake—as a book of personal history, anecdote (gossip), glimpses, questionings—as a soliloquy, one man talking, originally perhaps to himself only, but now for anyone to eavesdrop upon.

Could anything be more vulnerable? More presuming, self-conscious, arrogant? And at the same time, more humble, courageous, generous? Even if the author were not someone I esteem as a composer and love as a friend, I would be moved and respectful. I might flinch at the egotism, or frown at the assumption. But I would want to remember that some of this reaction is my own doing. "To have great poets," said Whitman, "there must be great audiences too." The same is true of vulnerable diaries.

But let me not seem to exaggerate. No—this diary is not at all the "total" book that Poe dreamed of—"My Heart Laid Bare." Nor does it sustain anything like Thoreau's "waking" tone of voice. But here and there it comes closer to those peculiar and dangerous ideals than—well, than any other book published in America during the past year. Is this fatuous talk? Am I doing Ned Rorem the disservice of staking untoward claims for what, after all, is only part of one man's very ego-prone diary? If so, I am eager to implicate myself in whatever impertinence or bad taste may be involved. For as truly and needfully as I trust in any kind of literature, or in any use of our language, I believe in this genre of book—unconditionally; and for this particular instance of that genre, I am, at the very least, grateful.

Let me put it this way. In the secular, pulverized world we live in today, some of us have little or no sense of community, of communion left. The forms may still be observable, in varying stages of atrophy or mimicry. But community itself is hard to come by. Yet whenever a writer, any writer, uses some semblance of his own first person and tells me something about himself or

the world around him which only he could have known, then
a viable community of two is formed as I read. It can be a
friend or a stranger. It can be my son writing a letter from his
prep school, or it can be Marcel Jouhandeau writing a diary
from a Paris suburb. Someone speaks and I listen. For a time we
make a whole greater than our separate parts. I may not like
what he tells me, I may not understand him. I may suspect him
of being a liar, or self-deceived. But there he is—one unanony-
mous, unsure, all-too-human *semblable*. If I am not too prudent,
I can hear him, join him, as Thoreau wanted to be joined. But
more than the literary art is involved, and I must bring more
than my safe aesthetic responses. The encounter may be joyous.
It may also be maculate, messy, perturbing, as human relations
so often are. And if I am merely afraid of perishing, and quote
Nietzsche's half-truth, is it fair to blame only the other party,
in this case, Ned Rorem? Won't I myself be at fault, too, in
my timidity, or "good taste," or tenuous pride?

—*Robert Phelps*

After lunch in the upstairs salon of the Vicomtesse
Marie Laure de Noailles. Included are, from left to
right, Ethel Semser (American soprano with whom I
was then preparing a concert); N.R.; Jacques Dupont
(painter); Marie Laure; Georges Geoffroy (*décorateur*)
and Jacques Février (pianist). (*Photo by Fémina*)

With Marie Laure at her country house.

HYÈRES, APRIL 1952

Oscar Dominquez, Marie Laure, N.R.

With Georges Auric who, during the summers, lived next door to us.

HYÈRES, 1953

Francis Poulenc. (*Photo by N.K.*)

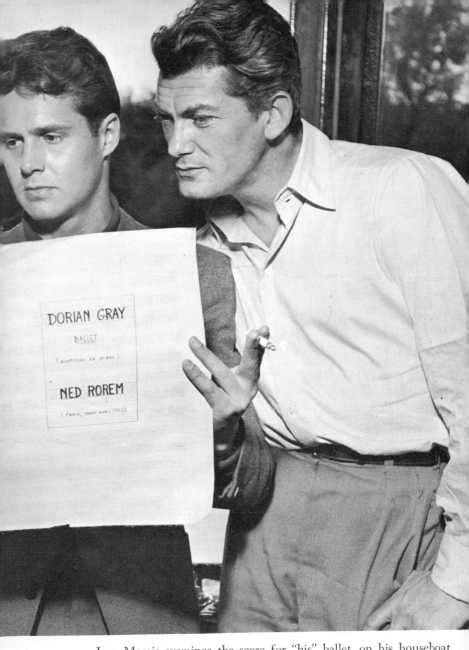

Jean Marais examines the score for "his" ballet, on his houseboat in the Seine, April 1952.

Jennie Tourel in Venice, where she sang Baba in the première of *The Rake's Progress*, September 1951.

With Aaron Copland. (*Photo by Herbert Kubly*)

With Virgil Thomson. (*Photo by Gianni Bates*)

Marie Laure in her entrance
hall, 11 Place des Etats-Unis,
Paris.

Picasso's version of Marie Laure
during the war. (*Collection:
Vicomtesse de Noailles, Paris*)

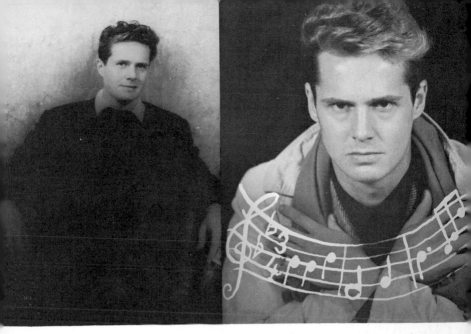

by Carl Van Vechten

by Man Ray

NED ROREM

by Jean Cocteau

by Henri Cartier-Bresson

Robert Wallenborn, N.R., Chloë Owen, Werner Egk, in Munich, April 1954.

Marie Laure, N.R., Madeleine Renaud, Jean-Louis Barrault, Hyères, July 1955.

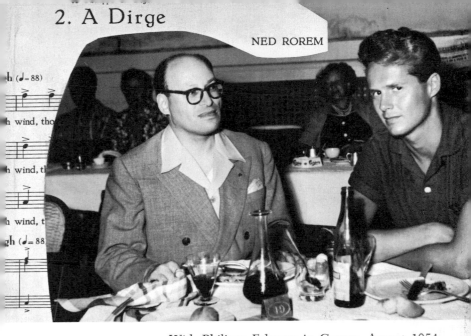

2. A Dirge

NED ROREM

With Philippe Erlanger in Cannes, August 1954.

With Muriel Smith in London, January 1954.

With Julien Green and Robert de Saint Jean (*far left*) at the first performance of my *Second Piano Sonata*, Théâtre des Champs-Elysées, February 1951. (*Photo by* Paris-Match)

With Julius Katchen, preparing the *Second Piano Sonata*, in Paris, 1951.

In Paris, March 1953. (*Photo by Henri Fourtine*)

In my room at Marie Laure's. (*Photo by Robin Joachim*)

N.R., Denise Bourdet, Boris Kochno, Comtesse Pastré, Jacques Février
in Hyères, 1954. (*Photo by James Lord*)

In Marie Laure's ballroom, Paris, June 1954. (*Photo by Claude Michaelides*)

At Père Lachaise cemetery, Paris, January 1954. (*Photo by Guy Bourdin*)

Part 1
Paris: May-July, 1951

> *No artist needs criticism, he only*
> *needs appreciation. If he needs criticism*
> *he is no artist.*—GERTRUDE STEIN

A stranger asks, "Are you Ned Rorem?" I answer, "No," adding, however, that I've heard of and would like to meet him.

Have been back in Paris over a week now. I'm never really happy here: not only because I drink too much and don't work very well, but also because I have no *chez moi* and am envious of all friends who do. It is spring with warm nights beautiful and sad. Most of the time I spend endlessly walking from quarter to quarter ("looking for love where it can't be found— waiting for love where it will not come"), and have memorized the entire city, knowing also where love *can* be found.

Lunch yesterday with Nora Auric and Guy de Lesseps. We talked of nothing but masturbation. Guy maintains that, yes, it *does* cause circles under your eyes, being an unshared act, an unbroken circle of sensations given to oneself with no true release.

Two years ago tonight (May 20th) I left New York for Le Havre, where the S.S. *Washington* arrived very early on a morning of screaming sea gulls and silver fog. France. And I looked toward the land knowing that deeper into it, behind those gutted buildings, lay the place where I would not have to bring myself. (Dr. Kraft had warned against the danger of displacement. He was wrong: displacement has made me new.) Very early, as on the morning of Christ's ascension, in a drizzle of gray toward a miniature country seemingly made of berets and real, live French stevedores, I descended from the boat, and my first long home has since become always the farthest away of dreams. The two months I'd planned to stay became two years, and may become two hundred.

The other day in Galignani's Julien Green bought me a beautiful Bible with gold-edge pages. Robert Kanters, browsing, saw us, and whispered to me: *"Quel puritain!"*

"Mais non," I replied, *"Tu serais étonné. C'est fou comme la Bible peut faire bander, elle aussi!"*

Youth is beautiful, age ugly. But is the wisdom of age beautiful? We know nothing old we did not know as children; we merely submit essentially unchanged reactions to a wearier refinement. I detest subtlety; I like strength. Strength is never subtle in art or in life.

This afternoon I met Picasso . . . Valentine Hugo had come to lunch, after which Marie Laure de Noailles sat me at the keys like a wise student to play my little pieces. Then Valentine (she who costumed Dryer's *Joan of Arc*) with her blond Anna May Wong bangs, bewitched by new blood, danced for me (at her age) *Le Sacre du Printemps* as she recalled it from that fatal day in 1913. . . . Later Marie Laure took me to a screening of *Los Olvidados* (Buñuel had, after all, been her *poulin*). We

arrived late in darkness. The somber finish unprepared me for
the coquettish tap on Marie Laure's shoulder when the lights
went up. We turned: it was Picasso. Those jet bullet eyes both
burned into my brain and absorbed me into his forever. I was so
carbonized I forgot their glib exchange. . . Later, with Jacques
Fath, we went to dine in the country *chez les Hersent,* and I
returned in time to meet Guy Ferrand's midnight train at the
Gare d'Austerlitz.

🌷

Jennie Tourel, never better, sang *Schéhérazade* at the Empire.
At *"ou bien mourir"* she threw her whole weight into the
audience!. . . Tea with Ciccolini. *Souper chez* Fulco Verdura,
Quai Voltaire.

I know I *can* compose and I know *how;* but I don't know *why*
I came to this instead of to sculpture or poetry, or perhaps even
dance. (Couldn't one kind of creator have been any other kind?)
After ten years of chattering every known musical speech, of
imitating now one and then another school, of wanting to
become famous by writing like the famous, I've decided now to
write again the way I did age eleven when I knew no one: *my*
music from *my* heart with *my* own influences. It's important to
be "better than," not "different from," and everyone has forgotten
how to write nice tunes.

I guess this music is really *French* at the core (though I steal
from Monteverdi occasionally, and pretty much from Bach
naturally—not to mention what I hear at the movies, what I hear
all around).

🌷

In New York I had already heard of Marie Laure de
Noailles; I was aware of both the lady and her attributes, and
on leaving for France in the spring of 1949 I was determined
to know her. I arrived like any other francophile tourist with

intentions of spending one summer. But from the outset that insular nation contradictorily greeted me with open arms: within a month I knew and—so much more important!—was known by most of the musical milieu.

My first meeting with Marie Laure took place that fall at the opera. Eager Henri Hell presented us. I said: "How do you do?" She turned her back. . . Second encounter: the Méditéranée restaurant. She, to Sauguet: *"Je ne le trouve pas si beau que ça."* Sauguet: *"Ah, non? Mais vous lui ressemblez beaucoup, chère amie.".* . . . Third time, *chez* Mme. Bousquet. Me: "I'm writing a ballet on your *Mélos* scenario for the Biarritz contest." She: "We'll see that you win it." And again turned her back.

After interludes in Morocco and Italy I returned to Paris for another siege early in '51. Then occurred my first contacts with Cocteau, Julien Green, Marie Blanche de Polignac, etc. But the Vicomtesse de Noailles remained *insaisissable.* One afternoon I learned she was to attend, that evening, a performance of *Yes Is for a Very Young Man.* I went, too, alone, in a black turtleneck sweater. I approached her and her companion Charles Lovett and we adjourned to the latter's apartment. Marie Laure was simultaneously cool, coy, and cultured; I, playing the ingenuous American. She invited me to lunch next day, to various events the following week, painted my two portraits (one pale blue as a *voyou,* the other dark green as a Satie student), and I felt I was *in.* . . A fortnight later we were to leave at dawn with Labisse for a month at Hyères. When I arrived for the departure at her house, 11 Place des États-Unis, they'd already left. This was the first of her endless "tests." So I got drunk with Boris Kochno (who was also to have gone) and we telegraphed to Hyères. (Such abject persistence has, hopefully, long since quit me: it's the prerogative of *le jeune arriviste.*) Marie Laure answered cordially that we should come down the following week, and we did.

There began our bizarre and fruitful friendship, our love

affair. The fact that we were both born under the sign of Scorpio is what finally converted her.

At first I behaved as I felt she wanted me to. She encouraged gaudy and exhibitionistic comportment, partly in defiance of her formal background, partly to give herself an identity with the post-surrealist gang she hung out with. For instance: a few months after we met (the night of July 4, 1951, to be exact) she gave me a party. It was to celebrate the première of my *Six Irish Poems* by the radio orchestra with soloist Nell Tangeman (whom Marie Laure hated: my soprano friends frustrated her because *she* couldn't sing). That *soirée* was undistinguishable from a hundred others I would attend over the years. A buffet, groaning with champagne and smoked salmon and apricot tarts, voraciously stripped to a skeleton by rich old dukes and pompous movie queens elbowing their best friends as though they'd been starving for weeks, while Marie Laure, with a Giocanda smile, looked on. I arrived brash, open-necked and, above all, young. By 3 A.M. I'd downed who knows how many magnums. Whereupon, in front of everyone, I approached the Vicomtesse, and with no conscious provocation gave her a whack that sent her reeling to the floor. *"Mais il est fou!"* they all screamed, as I was restrained by the *maître d'hôtel* and Guy Ferrand. But the noble hostess motioned for them to release me, then rose with a bemused stare of utter satisfaction: she had triumphed before her friends: somebody new *cared*.

LE TOUT PARIS. It is easy to become intimately acquainted with the inapproachable innermost snob-life of Paris. You need only know one member, and in twenty-four hours (which includes the attendance of a single party) you will know them all, because each individual of this group knows no one outside. There are only about seventy-five members (of which the musicians are the classiest), and of course it is simple getting intimate with seventy-five people in twenty-four hours. . . At a dinner offered by the delectable Mme. Hersent there was a discussion on new "motifs" for next season's Balls. Jacques Fath suggested that everyone come so completely disguised as to be unrecognizable. What inexhaustible boredom! I suggest that sixty-nine refugees from *la Place Blanche* be introduced into the grand salon and that *le Tout Paris* be told that these are other members incognito. Marie Laure proposes costumes so arranged that only a toe, a nipple, or a tongue be allowed to show. . . Such is their conversation.

❧

At fifteen I used to sit in school, scared at not knowing the answers (at being "dumb," hence conspicuous). For the night before, instead of doing my homework, I had been discovering love as thoroughly as I ever will. Were my classmates aware?

❧

Each time I go to Henri Hell's we hear again Ravel's *Poèmes de Mallarmé*. This is delicious music, music that can be eaten. Is it because my first association with Mallarmé was the word *marmelade*? André Fraigneau once wrote: *"Les oeuvres de Mr. Ned Rorem . . . ont la candeur éblouissante du plumage du cygne de Mallarmé. Très personnelles, elles sont pourtant autant d'oiseaux qui se souviennent de la France. . ."*

❧

I bite away my fingernails and cuticle, realizing I'm practicing a sort of autocannibalism. We shed our skin completely every seven years; and I'm sure that without knowing it, we eat our own weight of ourselves during our lifetime.

❧

One New York evening long ago, at Virgil Thomson's with
Maurice Grosser and Lou Harrison, the four of us planned to
dine in, and, as the maid was absent, we proposed preparing the
meal ourselves. So everyone bustled about. Everyone but me.
I stood around inefficiently not knowing how to behave. (I've
always disliked domestic cooperation.) Maurice, peeved by my
usual vagueness, handed me knives and forks, saying, "Here,
make yourself useful!" But Virgil piped, "Leave Ned alone! Ned
doesn't have to work. Ned's a beauty!"

Since birth I had lived by this slogan. I'll always be a spoiled
child, but will never lose track of to what extent. Nor, I pre-
sume, will Virgil. I was working for him then as copyist, in
exchange for orchestration lessons (every lucid word of which
I'll always remember) and twenty bucks a week—of which I
banked five! Such thrift impressed him, just as I was impressed
by *his* thrift with notes. And so I composed my first songs, with
an instinctive formal economy which I've since tried vainly to
recapture.

❧

> All great [artists] have robbed the
> hives of diligent bees and, paradoxically,
> genius might be said to be the faculty
> for clever theft.
> —ENID STARKIE, Rimbaud

My song "The Lordly Hudson" (1947) is dedicated to Janet
Fairbank, a kind and needed lady who died the day it was
published.

Everett Helm gave a Christmas party in 1946. But it was John
Edmunds who got all of us to write songs, and in their presentation as an "affectionate garland" to Janet, it was he who pre-
sided. After everyone had played his piece and Janet's initial
thrill was calmed, the performers each sang. We did my
"Alleluia"; then Romolo DiSpirito sang Poulenc. I had never

heard "C" before, and at the final words *"Oh ma délaissée"* when
Eva Gauthier began to weep, I began to compose as I often do
when my brain is befuddled (this time on hot punch). . . I went
to meet George Perle and played for him what I could remember
of "C." He retched! My guilt began. We drank a lot of beer
and went through a lot of music (mostly twelve-tone, and
Machault, on whom he was writing a thesis). But always "C"
kept running through my head, getting increasingly distorted—
more distant, changed. I'd heard it only once. . . When I woke
up it must have been Sunday. I wanted to write a song. The
two sections of "C" that I liked were the same that everyone
likes: *"De la prairie. . ."* and *"Et les larmes. . ."* I recalled that
Poulenc had skipped the voice a fifth to the ninth of a ninth-
chord. Naturally this had to be changed a little. But I'd forgotten
the tune, the rhythm. I looked around for a poem onto which
I could force my vague ideas, and though I was sick of using
Paul Goodman, I decided to borrow "The Lordly Hudson"
(which was called simply "Poem" at that time). I'd already once
made some not very successful notes for these verses but I threw
them out.

In one sitting I wrote the song. The composing, though
accompanied by a hangover, was not the *result* of a hangover.

Here's how I did it: deciding on 6/8 because that means
"water" I suppose, I first wrote the vocal phrases "home, home"
and "no, no"—skipping a seventh and rising in the sequence,
because Poulenc had skipped a fifth and dropped. Then I decided on the accompaniment pattern, and for the rest of the
words I simply used taste and a melodic stream of consciousness.
This can't be explained, but it's called "filling in" and sometimes
by accident it works. What I mean is that after the precipitating
inspiration of "home, home," all the rest was devised, often in
variation form (it goes without saying that "this is our lordly
Hudson" is merely an elaboration on "home, home").

Without any changes I gave it to Janet Fairbank who sang it

under the title of "Poem," then "Driver, What Stream is it"—
until Richard Dana said he would print it, and then Paul said
"call it 'The Lordly Hudson.'" We all think now it's his best
poem.

Any good song must be of greater magnitude than either the
words or music alone. I wouldn't mind if this piece were played
in concert on the violin; or, omitting the vocal line, as a piano
solo.

I was always embarrassed when I played this song over for
myself. It seemed too obvious, too schmaltzy. Like most composers I can't sing well, but I *can* be moved to tears when I sing.
And so I used to write for the voice everything I couldn't do,
until I realized that singing is the most natural of all expression.
Anything a composer can't sing well enough to please himself, he
shouldn't write. Of course when I had to sing it for others the
embarrassment began. But nobody said it was horrible, so I began
to like it (one can't continue to create well without being com-
plimented). Then it won a citation for being the best song of
1948 and so I have practically no more guilt. No one dreams
of the rapport with "C." (Is making a piece of art perhaps an act
of shy but aggressive guilt?)

In finishing, I must say there's a misprint in the tempo mark.
It reads: "Flowing but Steady—($\downarrow$ = 114)." Of course it should
be $\downarrow$ = 114, for as it stands now it wouldn't be flowing but a
whirlpool—nor steady, but jittery.

❧

It is *conscious* plagiarism that demonstrates invention: we are
so taken with what someone else did that we set out to do likewise. Yet prospects of shameful exposure are such that we disguise to a point of opposition; then the song becomes ours. No
one suspects. It's *unconscious* stealing that's dangerous.

❧

Yesterday I met Man Ray. I'd always mistakenly thought he was French. For twelve years I've admired his pictures of the French Great, of sadness or sadism (women chained in a court-yard living among their own excrement), pictures of people. These things nourished the legend we Americans are raised on, that celebrities are of different flesh than others. Yet Man Ray himself is a meek little man, not particularly interesting despite his myriad contacts. In fact all the great I've met have dis-appointed me: they are too concerned with their work to be personally fabulous. They are like anyone, they are like me. Well, then where *are* the myths that, as an American, I craved in my youth? They must, of course, be the movie stars (I have never known one). Gloria Swanson is great through her person and not through her work. It is she, then, whose clothes we rip off in the street to see if she exists (would we do the same for Gide, for Einstein?). Therefore I must know a movie star: Lana Turner or Dietrich. (The men don't count, they don't wear make-up.)

I'd rather have known Nijinsky, whom I've venerated since childhood, for he was what we all would like to have been: a flying man. But I did actually meet Barbara Hutton Troubetzkoy in flesh and blood.

She's a legend to all Americans of my generation because the inimitable Miriam Hopkins fifteen years ago made a movie about her called *The Richest Girl in the World,* and the movies are our history book. With my poet friends at twelve, lovers of immortal women, we would discuss for hours the sumptuousness of Miss Hutton's scandals, her jade screen. . . Later, in Tangier, I saw the house she'd built there, though I was told she never visited it.

Then one early evening recently, Marie Laure (because it is part of her profession, attending parties) took me to a "Cocktail" (as the French say) at the apartment of a Mr. Straus and wife

who spend their life looking out onto the Place Vendôme. I was
already high from a "Cocktail" at Mme. Bousquet's and one for
Aix at the Véfour (joyously leading the Parisian life I despise
in others), so that the apartment struck me as atrociously dreamy.
Decorated only in purple (and its offshoots) the spacious place
resembled a dignified funeral parlor: mauve bathroom and bed-
room with mauve curtains (which were drawn), mauve light
bulbs, sheets of lavender satin, and a dressing table with violet-
tinted mirrors into which Louise de Vilmorin observed herself
comb her hair. There was a flood of rosy-mauve champagne flowing from room to purple room, and in this flood floated dozens of
beautiful thirty-seven-year-old pink gigolos in which le Tout
Paris abounds. We stood dizzily at the window watching a pretty
purple sunset disappear behind the gray stone of the Ritz Hotel.
Then we drank more sparkling burgundy as the guests began to
thin out. Pretty soon I realized through a haze that I had been
left alone on a red velvet couch beside the liquor table where a
white butler kept pouring and pouring with an elegant sneer.
All was hushed. From a room I had not yet seen came the lan-
guorous strains of the Rosenkavalier waltzes. Suddenly people
began running in and out, nervously looking for smelling salts
and crystal-mauve cologne bottles, tearing their hair and ex-
claiming, "Oh, this time it's surely the end!" etc., while the
waltzes played sadly on. Finally Marie Laure came up to me
saying something like, "It's Barbara Hutton. She had a stroke and
is dying of stomach cancer in the next room." I was now allowed
to go in too, as long as I promised not to stare, to "act natural."
. . . There she was, dancing moodily with one of the forgotten
gigolos, the two of them trembling slowly in the middle of the
floor. She can't have weighed sixty pounds and her moronic eyes
oozed like black wounds from beneath an enormous hat. She fell
upon the couch in a daze and asked to be alone with me for a
moment, and though nobody liked that idea since I was not
famous and they would rather have worried about being natural

in front of Miss Hutton with smelling salts, etc., they acquiesced and went away to discuss her death. We talked about America and how nice we both were. Then everyone came back and I was forced to leave.

Afterwards, at about eleven, Marie Laure and I, each quite depressed, went to the Catalan for dinner during which there was a thunderstorm.

❧

What is music? Why, it's what musicians do! It's whatever a given listener feels it to be. It's any series of sounds and silences capable of moving at least one heart. It may move us, but won't change us. The experience of exposure to music may change us (though one may be exposed for years with immunity), but not the music itself; it can only awaken and make us more what we already are. Art has no ethical purpose and does not instruct. The same "message" can be reiterated by different artists but is most educational when least artistic (i.e. most literal).

What is *good* music? The music that is good for you, that disturbs involuntarily like an erection. Longevity is no pre-requisite since "good" is not an artistic but a moral ingredient. . . But *great* music doubtless does deal with Time, though not with decisions of the greatest number. The mass does not decide. If Michelangelo did create for a mass (debatable) his subject matter was the same as that of lesser artists. He was great not because of his material or mass appeal, but because he was Michelangelo. The masses don't know the difference. Ask them!

Until yesterday music's very nature was such that explanation was unimportant to appreciation (proof of the pudding was in the eating); today music's very nature is such that explanation is all-important to appreciation (like certain political polemicism which theorizes beyond proportion to reality). I say *appreciation* advisedly: *enjoyment* is now a niggardly, if not an obscene, consideration. That composition should need such verbal spokesmen indicates that, for the first time ever, the very essence of the art has changed. There's no more room for the *petit maître,* that "second-rater" (if you will) whose talent is to delight or, even sadly, to move his hearer to dance and sing. There is room for only masterpieces, for only masterpieces have the right to require the intellectual (as opposed to sensual) concentration and investigation needed for today's "in" music. Masterpieces are made by the few geniuses born each century. Yet hundreds now compose *in the genius style* while denigrating those who compose *what they hear*. Certain painting now is healthy if only because it's witty. Music, as always, trails humorlessly behind the other mediums.

The fact that music is scandalously received seems automatically to validate it for those afraid of ultimately being proved wrong.

Since we all must live in a cage (also the artist: without restraint he is not one), I prefer my own design. If I've not joined the avant-garde (henceforth called the Academy) it's not that I don't approve of—or even agree with—them; it's because of a terror of losing my identity. Still, I'm capable of arguing any view or its opposite, depending on who I'm trying to persuade what to.

I have just finished *Notre-Dames des Fleurs*. It's upsetting. Nobody reads Genet without suffering attacks of sexuality, and sincere, gross depression. But daily news reports of domestic crimes have the same effect on me (the wonderful Heirens trial in Chicago six years ago), and I cannot believe that Genet will be remembered.

For art is form, and also disguise. With him it is neither. How much more troubling is Jane Austen's torturous *lack* of orgasm, exquisitely wound in an air-tight tube, envied by the better detective-story novelists (*they* who are the writers of today).

Lesser French geniuses will last longer: Cocteau, because he knows where are Beginnings and Ends (art needs these); or Gide, because he knew that one does not write of love and crime in sexual description. Art is *greater* than being natural. It's concentration and suggestion.

But, oh, while it lasts, I quiver from the stimulus! (Though afterward I can do nothing with it.) I am told that in his film there is no *jouissance*—that it is touching.

In Washington, D.C., Glenn Dillard Gunn writes: "Rorem is the first successful modern romanticist."

If I am a significant American composer it is because I've never tried to be New. To reiterate: it's more pertinent to be Better than to be Different. American composers have the most dazzling techniques today; but they all have "masterpiece complexes" and write only symphonies. I believe I shall be ever more tempted to write just songs (the forgotten art) with as few notes as possible.

At Jacob's Pillow years ago a Mrs. Derby told my fortune. The cards said I had wasted myself since very early; that I'd never exerted my full potentialities because of another equally strong blocking force. But it was not too late to choose between good and evil: growth of music, or ethical deterioration.

Picasso says *"que l'artiste qui se répète n'a été qu'une fois artiste."* He is wrong, and for himself as well. We all have but one obsession, though it can show itself in different ways. . .

Eyes askew and wild hair! The only time I ever met Wanda Landowska was long ago when I went to show her my harpsi-

chord concertino. No sooner had I entered than she took the pins
from her hair, which fell in waves to her waist. "Take it," she
said, "take it in handfuls and pull it, pull it *hard!* and never go
tell people I wear a wig!"

Her first words to D. P. had been: "You look so *sympathique*,
young man! Are you a pederast?" *"Oui, Madame."* "Good. Now
let's talk about music!"

Every day I find myself wondering in what manner I'll finally
die. Of course, I am convinced that it will be violent, unpleasant,
and soon, either by the hand of a friend near the Boulevard
Clichy (though, unfortunately, I never take chances unless
drunk, and drunks are never murdered)—or in a concentration
camp for vaguer reasons, and by tortures of which one does not
speak (this I wouldn't be able to avoid by will). . . Perhaps I
write this from fear, knowing that what is written does not
occur. I feel that I shall die in "a certain way" before I grow old;
I'm not sure of it and don't want it but I feel it. I have no idea
if this will be by trade or war for the two things are equal in
my soul. . . Some people just *do* die in certain ways: Julien
Green will die in a certain way, as did Maurice Sachs and Jean
Desbordes; Henri Hell will not, nor Xénia, nor did Gide nor
Dino Lipatti (though he was very young, like Mozart, like Janet
Fairbank). Bérard died in what I call a certain way. Boris
Kochno wants to but probably won't. Other people just die,
whether they are young or old. It's hard to explain why. Some-
times we are quite surprised.

Death is a private affair, and the secret of its duration (when
we learn it) should never be divulged. A friend said (rather
ingenuously, I feel) that far from fearing death he hoped for
total lucidity at the end so as to savor that supreme moment. . .

Really there's no relation between life and the death which so illogically concludes it. Lucidity? What difference if we are in a coma?—comas are part of life. The pearly gates won't be appreciable through a state which in life we name *lucid*.

And that friend continued: "You too are dying already from birth, and any stranger passing in the street carries off a shred of you in his memory.". . . I feel we live when we live and die when we die and those facts are unrelated. If strangers steal my shreds, don't I steal theirs? Who gives without taking? Sometimes I even feel quite swollen (though the earth, I believe, keeps its own weight). Is a *chef d'oeuvre* the less beautiful, the more old, for the million pairs of eyes that have converged upon it?

❦

Socrate of Satie. Yesterday I sang it through to myself for the first time since I bought it along the *quais*. (I later stole an old copy from Marie Laure, dedicated to Valentine Hugo in Satie's remarkable hand; this is one of my treasures.) I first heard it around eight years ago when Virgil Thomson sang it for me at a piano in the New Jersey countryside. All the 1920-Paris-New Yorker's had a copy, sacred as the Bible but infinitely rarer, just as Falla's Harpsichord Concerto is the golden calf of young South Americans. But I wasn't able to really know Satie's *Socrate* (Plato's I'd forgotten and known and reforgotten) until last fall. As I had no piano, Michel Girard let me come to work at his house every afternoon (that is where I wrote *Mélos*). The first day I arrived alone into this most beautiful home in Paris, 56 rue de Varenne, with the best piano in France, high ceilings, and three nervous incestuous Dachshunds with Wagnerian names. I had on my famous Kelly-green sweater. A servant gave me a Coca-Cola, then left me with the dogs beneath the high ceilings and my new score of *Socrate* with which I sat down on a velvet piano stool and began to sight-read. . . I seldom come across more than one new work a year which upsets me, for masterpieces are quickly known if one is starved, and my adolescence was an impatient one. I think that every musical and literary work that I love most today, I knew and loved at seventeen. Because a receptive person discovers early what he seeks, and his inclinations rarely change. . . Being Norwegian, I don't often cry. But when Michel came home that Monday night he saw me at the piano, a green stain smeared with tears at Socrates' death. Julien and Robert de Saint Jean (who live next door at 52 *bis*) then showed up to dine that night and we talked of nothing else. I remember I got very drunk on *marre*. It's hard to know at the instant who is the more moving: Plato or Satie. Hugues Cuénod, though he sings this work marvelously (so "whitely"), feels that much of it is arbitrarily, not inevitably, monotonous. . . Yes, *Socrate* is a piece for composers: we all know it by heart and sing it to each other but it never has a public performance.

I permit people to think they're "communicating" with me, but they aren't really. I need their love, not their complicity. Yet whatever happens to me—that I *allow* to happen to me—is my life. Tomorrow, in six weeks, in ten years will I be reconciled to dying? Do we never change? Are we indeed *alive?* or is that word an invention?

Nadia Boulanger, to everyone in the musical world and to thousands out of it, is the most remarkable pedagogue of our century, and perhaps (who knows) of all time. I've just come from a necrophilic representation at *l'église de la Trinité*. Lili's funeral is more or less restaged there annually, to an accompaniment of her compositions performed with taste. Each guest is greeted with a tear-stained smile by Nadia Boulanger. Now I know why she is as she is.

Had Lili (surely far from greatness) not died thirty years ago, her acutely Roman sister might today be unknown. Certainly in those early days Nadia's *soeur cadette* was her dearest thing, so that young death was hence a canonization. Nadia has since profitably devoted her maiden life to a shadow with substance. Her sister having been her final treasure, she's ever after shunned all others of that sex (all but those stooges who *solfège* like machine guns but have the talent of octopi), and symbolically espoused each gentle youth in her vicinity. This she accomplishes as only a strong and pious woman could: by fortifying the myth of technique. Only a female (and uncreative) could have built within herself the most spectacular musical métier in the world today. Hers is the search for a true spark among those crackling in her synthetic electricity, a shimmer attracting others who fear to make love.

This shimmer exploded into flame just before the war, in Boston, where she was the chief guide for any composer anywhere (a prejudiced guide, of course: all great spirits are). Though I'm told she'd already begun to long again for countesses at her command.

The flame's extinction (if such it may be called) came in the late forties when the new young Americans emigrated to Paris like good shepherds bearing dubious gifts. But they found (with the change of air) they didn't now need her. Does she know she's been cheating herself for thirty years? Nothing's more tragic than a teacher. She was a grand one.

Now, at her "Wednesdays," she moves like an automaton with still enough oil in its unreal veins to provide transfusions for certain human ladies. But the boys? Who was her prize? Jean Françaix? How can she help but resent the creative male too, the robber who, with her help, stole her sister's genius?

Realizing her notable lack of gift she has herself become a

countess. She *receives,* and in a manner unrivaled for quaintness. Along with her yearly memorial for Lili she offers a weekly wake for her own virginity. She has been generous in her masochism and it has often been fruitful. One observes the fruits each Wednesday at the wake. "No, it's worse than a wake," says Xénia, "for at wakes they feed you!"

❦

My visit to Cocteau—to "the inspired Jean," as Paul Goodman calls him—was paid last Friday at eleven in the morning. A perfect, sunny day. I was in a state of terror which wouldn't have taken hold if I had just been going to see him cold. But I'd written him a warning of my approach in two flirtatious letters (snapshots of myself enclosed), and received eloquent and equally flirtatious replies.

He lives at 35 rue Montpensier in a smallish and very low-ceilinged apartment overlooking the Palais-Royal garden, the hordes of playing children, and the Véfour restaurant. (He can wave to Colette who lives on the same courtyard, but he spends most of his days now with his friend—Paul, from the film of *Les Enfants Terribles*—in the country at Milly; he can work nowhere else.)

He opened the door himself, and immediately showed me into a tiny room at the right where he followed, locking the door, after telling the maid not to bother us for two hours. This tiny room had a tiny bed with a scarlet spread piled high with books, prints, current art and literary magazines, none of the pages of which was cut, a desk and a drafting table (each also piled high with books), a telegraph set (out of order), and a blackboard reaching to the ceiling, on which was a chalk drawing by Jean of a boy's profile, a Siamese cat (female). . . Cocteau himself wore a floor-length sky-blue dressing gown cut like a medieval priest's; the sleeves completely covered his hands, though his gestures were so violent that I caught frequent glimpses of the longest fingers I have ever seen. His voice had no relation to the one we've heard at the movies: it sounded rather higher; he talked incessantly. He didn't sit down once, but continually paced the little room, occasionally petting the cat in passing. His favorite words are *con* and *emmerder*, and he scarcely makes a sentence without one or the other. Yet everything about the congested atmosphere was elegance itself: none of those crumbling corners one finds in even the grandest French homes.

At no time did I feel the hot, lazy, demoralizing magic which proved so fatal for Maurice Sachs during his friendship with Cocteau twenty years ago. Nor did I find him beautiful. He did strike me as more "sincere" than I would have guessed, and *au fond* has the tone of a real artist. From his social style (that of an actor) I have no reason to believe that the identical conversation was not repeated with the next admiring young American who came to call. . . Nevertheless I tried to talk as much as I could, and as he ends every phrase with a brutal *quoi* or *hein*, it's impossible not to answer. Each time I said something with which he agreed, he would roll it up into a "cliché" (a *formule*, the French say) and throw it back to me. Though we seemed almost always in accord (far from passively) I can think of no one who might fatigue me more, so stereotyped has he become, as though he were before one of his own mirrors! He had the graciousness to ask if I'd learned French as a child along with English. On learning I'd been speaking it just a year, he feigned astonishment.

We spoke *en somme* of three things: how, why and where the creator does or should create; how a possible war should effect a creative person; sex and crime in American cities (other than New York). . . Creating is like shitting; indeed, this was the image he used. *"Quand j'ai chié mon Orphée,"* though he might have said, "when such an idea fell from heaven," which for me would be more expedient. The artist must grow ever more selfish, must never seek to rearrange the world. *"Il doit s'en foutre des guerres. . ."* Like all the French, Cocteau is more amused than fascinated by Doctor Kinsey (and by psycho-analysts).

I forgot to ask if his star came off an alchemist's hat, and if he used it when signing checks.

Is a fugue the pointless conversation of persons in too-perfect agreement? Or someone insane talking to himself?

Part 2
Hÿères: July, 1951

We arrived here at three this morning, Marie Laure and I, hideously out of sorts. Fifteen hours by car during which the only interesting sights are when passing through Lyon, the one French city that intrigues me. It's closed and cold and terrible, and despite its lack of art, the black mass is still celebrated here if one knows how to find it. Seemingly endless miles of *quais* bordered with seven-story buildings (without elevators), all identical in the evening sunlight. And wasn't it in Lyon where George Perle, once during the war, entered a *pissotière* and, looking down, saw there in the urine a decapitated human head?

The night before leaving Paris it seemed as if I had already gone. This was Friday. As always before quitting the great city I took a long walk, this time going far up by *l'Observatoire*. Of course I knew something would happen, since Experiences on the eve of a departure are inevitable (and become more meaningful than similar occurrences at other times, when one can reject or postpone them. Love is Resignation, which means an incident one does not know how to postpone). So, almost to Boulevard Montparnasse, I hear feet and then a bespectacled young man stops me. Would I like to visit his home and *"bavarder un peu"*? He lives on the third story of a house on the darkest street in Paris. I find myself in a huge room lined with books, at least ten thousand books, and all in Russian. My host is a professor of that language, and I eat two small oranges and drink a cup of very good coffee (as I have walked a great deal). It is midnight. Then the guessing game begins; it is always the same. "You have a slight accent; may I ask if you are of foreign origin?" (This question inevitably followed by: "You must be a student *aux Beaux Arts!*") I hate these interrogations which give me a personality when I would prefer to remain anonymous; anonymity and lack of profession make the game more exciting (not to mention getting it over quicker, which is convenient if one has things to do early next day. In strictly anonymous encounters I generally play a role as far removed from my "natural" one as I can manage: this stimulates me). I almost say I am Dutch (that is what I'm most often taken for), then decide this is too revolting, and admit to being American, his Russian books notwithstanding. He says that although he's an accomplished linguist, English is the one language he could never learn—which gives me a feeling of superiority. I decide to tell him I have read *Stavrogin's Confession* and also Gogol, and that Prokofiev made an opera out of *The Nose* (though it may have been Schostakovitch who made it a ballet, but in any case my host wouldn't have known). He falls out of his seat, since until then I have said almost nothing and he has taken me for the anonymous nonprofessional. . . I tell him I am deeply fond of Russian literature; that I feel I have a French soul; that, although I read much less now than when I was fourteen, my taste has not changed and probably never will; that I feel that people whose taste changes have no taste; that I am twenty-seven (he had obviously taken me for younger).

Now he no longer finds me a stray cat ("stray cat" is what he said) and I feel he is drawn to me, and as I consider this a weakness, I become bored. Therefore I use his phone to call Marie Laure and speak in English to increase the mystery. Marie Laure advises me to go to bed soon as we're leaving early. On hanging up I tell the Russian teacher that the woman with

whom I've spoken has told me to retire early and that I must
therefore leave. This is dangerous, since there is nothing sadder
than the parting of a brand new friend, and had he been a
maniac or something (they never are) he would have killed me
on the spot. I say I am a composer, and he gives me a green
leather edition of *Anna Karenina* as I have never read it (on
reaching home I inscribe it myself). I leave, but to my aggrava-
tion he decides to accompany me as far as Boulevard St. Germain.
There we say goodby. . . It is a beautiful summer night of the
kind that only happen in big cities. . .

On the rue de Rennes I come across Bel-Amich, who says
where did I get that book at such an hour, as he had seen me
walking by earlier and I wasn't carrying any book. We go for
hot milk on a café terrace and, as I am telling him where I got
the book, a man at the next table asks me for a light, and while
I am giving it to him he strokes my hand and whispers can he
see me tomorrow. His face is pleasing, but I answer that alas I
cannot as I'm leaving town (forgetting the danger once again,
that the parting of a brand new friend, etc.). He says he has
never seen eyes like mine, gives me an address, asks me to write.
Marie Laure thinks I should.

It's during the mornings that I try to do my composing here,
but I'm finding it difficult to get back into the habit: to write
something that is more than "well made" and which ignores the
surroundings. . . Every day at eleven Thérèse, *la bonne,* comes
into the music room where I am attempting to work, and brings
me a tray of coffee. She doesn't say a word and steals out quickly,
for she thinks I am a genius and is respectful (not wishing to
disturb my inspiration with her worldly presence). This amuses,
but at the same time worries me, as Thérèse knows less than I
how feeble are my efforts at this moment. And if I cannot work
well, then I have not the right to eat.

Alcohol, like sex, is an end in itself. But art is not. For artists art unfortunately isn't enough. Our gifts aren't necessities, they're luxuries we're chained to.

I have allowed Marie Laure to read this book and she says I have a childlike quality. This delights me, for in my heart my outlook has never advanced beyond that of a seven-year-old. *Et tant mieux!* I know no artist who thinks with the realistic disillusionment of adults. I met Picasso once and then for an instant: he was very old, but his presence dazzled with the enthusiasm and naïveté of an infant.

The quiet of the Midi is exhilarating, and Marie Laure an almost ideal companion (I would not have believed it). We have been just the two of us now for days, and we work like insects. *Mélos* is finished. At night we read (I Gogol, she detective novels) or we talk about wars, and the martyr Jean Desbordes whose eyes were ripped out and beetles put in. . . I play *Socrate* three times daily, and I orchestrate. Also I'm posing for the third picture of my life. Still, there are dramas: either the dog Diego has trembling fits, or Boris Kochno, being drunk, frightens us, as we are all alone on a country estate. . . The other day they asked me why I did not like the English and I said because one cannot tell the men from the women: the race has so crumbled that the sexes have merged and there is no further relationship between the modern Englishman and Shakespeare, between the modern Englishwoman and Jane Austen.

What is more loathsome than a totally educated man? I think no genius (at least in our day) is really well acquainted with arts other than his own. Kafka hated music. Painters know nothing besides painting. An artist does not *need* the other arts. A visit to a gallery sterilizes me, but even a bad concert is my inspiration.

❦

Marie Laure took my measurements (lying on my back, arms outstretched) and found them to be according to the classic golden law.

❦

In my new canary-yellow shirt (from Chez Vachon in St. Tropez), my golden legs in khaki shorts, my tan sandals, and orange hair, I look like a jar of honey.

Paul Eluard and his wife Dominique have come over from St. Tropez to spend the evening and the night. In expectation I panicked, as I always do when I must meet somebody new, even the janitor's daughter. As always happens, it passed more easily than I would have thought. For Eluard is all ease and quiet beauty. He is deeply sun-tanned (they had spent the afternoon on Ile du Levant, the land of nudists), has white hair, a black sweater, and an elegant voice. To him the Word is All—only the human voice has real meaning. Therefore Poulenc's rendering of his poetry into song leaves him cold, as he does not recognize the music he had heard when writing the verses, nor can he understand the word when sung (at least if it's Bernac, he says). He likes declamation; he likes *Socrate* and *Pélléas*. . . But a musician must never speak too long with a poet since they are both making the same thing (all art is the singing of old songs with new words) in unrelated ways; to each his own device is the more important, though he may admit the other's is more moving. . . After dining we sat on the terrace and he read us Baudelaire ("La Madonne") and a half-hour's worth of his own poems in that magnificent slow speech of tragedians. I am still not sure that poetry should be read aloud. But how the French love their language! They will say, for instance, of

Racine, "He writes beautiful French"; whereas *we* say, "Shake-speare writes beautifully.". . . Eluard feels that all creators are women in men's bodies, that he himself has a woman's instincts: *"Je me sens femme pénétrée"*: that it is therefore natural that they seek to sleep with men, or with the various substitutions of men found in real women. Artists like himself or like Picasso who prefer women, he considers abnormal: *"Picasso et moi, on est des vieilles gousses!"* He thinks it better to be drunk than sober; maybe he's right. I have always felt it unimaginative to want the head clear in order "to see things as they are."

Cocteau says all creators are half man and half woman, and that the woman is insupportable.

Coincidence: Mme. Eluard lived from 1941 to '44 in Fez at the Hôpital Cocard where Guy worked for years and where I visited daily. . . She has now gone to the tower studio and is asleep. I am alone up in my room. The night is stifling (this fourteenth of July without firecrackers) so my windows are wide open and I can hear Marie Laure and Eluard still down on the terrace drinking cognac. It's very sad. They are talking about *me*.

This evening I told Marie Laure innocently (though I real-ized it was the malicious result of strange and logical images passing before me since morning) of a letter to my mother in which I explained that our relationship was "strictly platonic." She was thunderstruck; and I, nonplused by her reaction. After a half-an-hour of restraint she fell into spasms of tears, and I grew aware of my crime. Can one have his mother and another woman at the same time without unhappiness? If the woman is happy, the mother is not, and vice versa. My ignorance had wounded, and the scene which followed shook me. . . Later we had a long whimsical talk on the nature of family structure, with the kind of fresh and precipitating inspiration that comes after vomiting.

The Eluards (of which he the wife, she husband) left us this morning; tomorrow the whole Auric clan arrives. And the peace of Hyères becomes like the nervous last scene in *Petrouchka* where bear overlaps nursemaid in the snow and everybody dances.

Why must we know so many people? Because any single person has his limits. One will begin to repeat himself after ten minutes, another after ten days, a third after three months, and a very sly one after a year. Sooner or later we know them all, and all their secrets. Each goes in his orbit, a cycle of subtleties which are our own and which we have known since the age of two. Each of our *clichés* becomes new insofar as we expose it to a new person. But *we* stay the same. Therefore no two people on earth are sufficient unto themselves.

Julien Green is obsessed by statues. Not just in his novels; but also, from one standpoint, his conversation and life may be said to consist of little else (like myself, he is essentially Protestant—despite his Catholicism—and therefore suspicious of the slightest motion of his little finger). . . One day, while walking together through the Tuileries, on our way home from one of the innumerable Paris teashops of which only Julien knows the whereabouts, he told me that once he had a plaster cast made of one of the half-life-sized Apollos from the Louvre. But he had toyed with it so much that it had finally collapsed. . . He then told me he used to have a friend—a fifteen-year-old Swedish writer of bad verse—who fell in love with one of the statues in this very garden (by the fountain near rue Cambon). One evening during the war he arranged to get locked in the garden, whereupon he raped the statue all night long, and then fell out of love. . . Julien says that his idea of Paradise is to be alone in a room full of nothing but beautiful statues. And I, being American, quite understand the fear of all that is flesh.

�','

Love implies a soldering anonymity which repels me. Or did. . . I am never *with* anyone, *anyone*—but nobody knows, because my barriers are made of glass. . . Quarrels in France strengthen a love affair, in America they end it.

🌱

Once we've defined a thing, the thing is frozen, breathes no longer. To "know" is to be sterile. To "look for" is to be young. All artists are by definition children, and vice versa.

🌱

She spoke:
"When I was a little girl we spent summers on a farm where I had a passion for physical cruelty, in spite of attempts at self-control. Hating myself, I used to go mornings toward the roost and kick the chickens from their sleep, leaving them helpless on the floor to squawk and flop. I then went smiling for breakfast, my young father blaming the crime onto foxes or snakes. . . As a farm girl I experienced a constant turning turmoil as I carved spears from hard birchwood, for I never enjoyed inflicting pain; I simply could not help it. Yet the desire enlarged for acts against animals. I'd just destroyed barnyard birds, but wished now to injure mammalian creatures. A strong decision—but I had strength of character! . . I meditated. I was going to maim the horse. A perfect horse he was, with a sleek black back, thick-legged and masculine, and gentle intelligence. Day after day I dreamed in my hayloft which afforded a view over this horse's stall, a small manger where it was impossible to turn completely around. Day after sunny day in the dark of the barn I took my six sharp birch spears; my precocious intention was to thrust

these into six parts of the horse: the two eyes, the nose, the spine, the genitals, the mouth. . . And I looked down onto the horse, watching his elegant male motion. An hour passed. I looked down, and two more hours went by, and my nervous perspiration dampened the hay with a smell of sick terror. And I tensed, and took one of my spears and sunk it deeply between the animal's shoulders. (I wanted, you see, I *wanted* this horse to *pay attention* to me!) Fright. He reared foaming and bellowed and shook and couldn't escape, quivering as he was with hurt. And I, fearful, slid from the loft and began running from the barn, but at the door stopped to look back. The horse was upright, shaking, his hooves crossed upon the gate of his stall, and large tears flowed on his face. And he said: 'Little girl, don't run away or be afraid. If I reared up it was only because the pain of your weapon shocked me so. I was not going to hurt you. O, come back.'. . . But I walked from the barn, and went slowly into the hills that surrounded my young father's farm. Here I sat beneath a pine and felt absolutely nothing and breathed the odor of needles and cones. Far below I could see the barn and still hear howling as the horse tried to extract the spear from his back. Then the noise became more and more feeble until it died away all together. . . But like unexpected thunder an insane shriek occurred and I knew the horse had forced himself through the wooden doorway. I waited for his revenge. But he went free, escaped to die, whinnying off through the trees in the *opposite* direction instead of galloping over to stamp out *my* small life."

The Aurics are daily visitors since they live next door. Nora has given me a marvelous Mexican shirt (cream and lavender brocade), and Georges took me to visit his mother, age eighty, to whom he recounted the first time he ever saw me: in June, 1949, I had just arrived in France, and was sitting late on a bar stool at La Reine Blanche, ordering innumerable cognacs with innumerable admirers and singing themes from *Le Sang d'un Poète* to Auric who spoke no English. Two years later such behavior would seem undignified, to my great, great sorrow.

❦

Last night we had a *bouillabaisse* which I couldn't touch because of the terror in its preparation. The secret is to throw live sea creatures into a boiling pot. And we saw a lobster who, while turning red in his death, reached out a claw to snatch and gobble a dying crab. Thus in this hot stew of the near-dead and burning, one expiring fish swallows another expiring fish while the cook sprinkles saffron onto the squirming.

❦

How old was I? ten? eleven? when I wrote Jean Harlow requesting her autograph. She answered: "To Ned Rorem with sincere best wishes—cordially, Jean Harlow." For years afterwards I signed my letters "Cordially."

❦

Late last night, on returning from an adventureless evening in Toulon with Raffaello, I found this note from Marie Laure slipped under my door:

My own beloved Ned,

I think I must explain why I love you so much. You are the total expression of what I have loved or still love in fragments. My whole life seems to have been a drive with pitchfalls [sic] towards you: marriage, children, lovers, friends and that ever-lasting quest of beauty and refusal of ugliness: my only conception of God or the universe. You are a little more than sex, a little more than childhood, much more than nature, and more than death; for if I died, my ghost would still haunt you, more living than any other alive female. Whatever you do, whatever

I do, whatever happens I will always love you because I have loved you and you are also more than time and space. For the space in which you move is beauty and the time music. And what is at the moment of beauty will always be. So sleep well my love.

(signed with her famous "leaf" insignia)

Evenings here we play four-hand music, the *Epigraphs Antiques*—or I play the phonograph: my skillful string quartet, or old Ella Fitzgerald records which remind me of Olga and the summer iciness of Lake Michigan where I first learned what an orgasm was. We also drink cider (I've had not a drop of liquor for nine days). . . And in the morning I begin to read alone with my (famous Noailles-type nearly-American) breakfast, so that I can't smartly realize the difference between my book and my dream.

Being myself a coward, a cheat, a weak-kneed opportunist, stingy and dishonest—I despise these things. Yet I have scant respect for courage and find that nine times out of ten it's the result of dullness or vanity. Not to cheat is to ignore love. I must admit that strong legs are exciting to behold, but I always walk swiftly, and besides I could strangle you if I so desired (still I've always been afraid, nearly ashamed of my strength. I know why.). . . Creative men have always known where to look; this is what makes them seem selfish on the first level, but on the second (and on all the following rungs as far as the sky) they are the most generous of all. Sincerity is the virtue of tiny folk; I prefer a many-faceted personality. . . Yet how long can this go on, since I continue to detest myself because my motives are irreconcilable.

In finishing *Opium* I wondered first, and especially, how Cocteau could have corrected the proofs of a book that flows with such improvisatory swiftness. But he did. Today he speaks with as equal intimacy of Proust, Debussy and Diaghilev, as he does of flying saucers; he wants it to be said in one hundred years that he embraced all. He would like also that there be a confusion of epochs about him, that people say, "But when exactly *did* he live, anyway? His life span seems to have been gigantic." At the same time, today, he receives countless young fans since he feels he's beginning to be forgotten as a person. Like Chaplin, he's exceeded the permitted glory (*"il a dépassé la gloire permise,"* as he himself said of Picasso) and become immortal during his lifetime. He therefore quite naturally never listens to anyone else, as there's no one else to listen to.

Oscar Dominguez maintains he's seen three flying saucers, but of course this is impossible, since not only is he nearsighted (I myself have known what glasses are since thirteen), a surrealist, and an alcoholic, but he has no religion. I like to think of flying saucers as holy stars announcing the Rebirth. Today is the first moment in the world's billion-yeared history that we have had a universal poem. And it is a beautiful one.

Lunch at Charles de Noailles's in Grasse. Cocteau is the only other guest. He speaks of Garbo. "Because she has carte blanche she only goes where she's not invited. Last week in Paris she knocked unexpectedly at my door. I was busy, *mais que voulez-vous?* there's only one Greta. I took her to eat at Véfour. In her baby French and my baby English we talked of how sad, how sad that she was afraid to mime the Phèdre that Auric and I created for her last year. After coffee she vanished into the afternoon. Next day I lunched alone, again at Véfour. The headwaiter asks: 'Monsieur Cocteau, that lady yesterday—was

it Madeleine Sologne?' I explain it was Garbo. 'Well,' he replies,
'I knew it was *someone* like that!'"

🌻

Garbo today might be hailed with—*cheers of disappointment.*

🌻

Julien, in his agitation, persists in referring to Marie Laure
as Marie Blanche, and then blushes. *"Tu rougis,"* I say to him.
And Marie Laure adds, *"Et moi, il me blanchit."*

🌻

And there was the alcoholic who, two hours before he was to
be burned at the stake, began drinking (from a bottle bribed
from the jailer—to lessen pain—though just a little) to such an
extent that memories of all the other sad and happy liquor
debauches teemed up around him. So in his execution he was
consumed in a sparkle of nostalgia, not to mention burning
quicker because of the brandy in his stomach.

🌻

What disappoints in Sade is his lack of obsession (I've just
thumbed through *Les 120 journées de Sodome*); as a matter of
fact he's rather gay. He's too general; whereas it's precision,
singularity, choice, which makes a pervert. When I have finished
the sexual act (as I see it), I say silently to the other: thank you
for having allowed me—without anger—to think my very special
thoughts. . . When I was little I thought that "intellectuals"
never made love—that they could never be troubled by what
troubled me. (They played the harpsichord, so how could they
hear dirty jokes?) I do not know, and am afraid of what's often
called Life; I avoid experience, which nevertheless hurls itself
at me. Yet I have memories. Unfortunately nostalgia cannot be
manufactured consciously, or I would go have a picnic at the

suburban zoo with a close friend just to remember this pleasant day years hence.

What have I done in my weeks of Hyères? I read fourteen books; went to a mediocre Aix performance of *Figaro* with Marie Blanche de Polignac, Robert Veyron-Lacroix, and Jacques Février (the first and third of whom stagger to a point where it's sure they'll each live fifty more years: their habits are strong as statues'); saw, and was saddened by (as always with great men, knowing their pain to be as ordinary as mine) Eluard again, this time in the distasteful town of St. Tropez; became a lush yellow-tan so that Robert said as I ate my fruit, *"Tu as l'air d'être une pêche qui en mange une autre"* (but I ate raw carrots too, for, like an alcoholic, I care for my health); orchestrated, orchestrated, and orchestrated; almost finished my *Five Eclogues*; wrote stacks of letters; became even closer to my dear Marie Laure; lunched with Poulenc who, with Auric, becomes less and less sure of himself and manifests this by speaking of the inadequacies of others: they both want to change, whereas if they stayed the same they might become great. (I am sure that each of *"Les Six"* dreads the day when one of them will die: the others will say, "Ah! at least it wasn't me this time; nevertheless it's beginning!" Moral: If death worries you, don't associate yourself with others. . . Unfortunately Margaret Truman is the same age as I, and I must go through life being the same age as she; even if she dies first, nothing can stop the awful fact that I'll die second.)

Famous last words of Ned Rorem, crushed by a truck, gnawed by the pox, stung by wasps, in dire pain: "How do I look?" It's harder to maintain a reputation for being pretty than for being a great artist.

Part 3

Fez, Morocco: August, 1951

Yesterday Guy Ferrand and I passed the day swimming with Henri Lhébrard (and friend) on the wild beach of Safi. The only other bathers were a group of native whores taking Sunday off from the town brothel. While their boy friends played a sort of baseball with a tin can, the whores (naked) dressed up in seaweed to attract our attention. But the baseball was also to attract our attention: that is how Morocco is made.

On the road to Safi are more camels than anywhere in the world. A camel has terrific strength; he can take off your arm with one bite. The leg bones are of unshatterable steel built to combat outrages rampant before history. . . A car—a "baby Simca"—can smash into a camel and be reduced to smoking crumbs; a few moments after, the camel, unscratched, stands off to consider the wreckage, chewing calmly, and smiling his bovine smile of stupid disdain. . .

Jean-Claude is also here in Fez. Yesterday he took me and Robert Lévesque up the mountain far behind our house to see a dead horse he'd found there some days ago. Lodged in a sort of stone pit, this exquisite sight was in a state of shocking putrefaction and smelled like nothing on earth. White worms and newly-hatched flies crawled from all directions toward the cadaver from which perforated intestines emerged. The horse (a mare, we concluded) seemed to have fallen from a height of twelve feet and broken its neck. The unexpected descent had deposited her quite prettily (meaning quite naturally) on the ground. Her legs—slim and now practically bone, making the hooves look enormous—were dainty as a dancer's, and the head was wonderfully twisted, eyes to the soil, in an attitude of modesty. This scene was the sole rupture in a fifty-mile desert of pebbles. So I recalled my first knowledge of death: that disemboweled cow in the vacant lot on our way to school in Chevy Chase's second grade; we kids then all dressed up as cows to counterfeit our wonder, our terror.

Lévesque, without further ado, began reciting Baudelaire's "La Charogne," but before he had finished we noticed coming over the hill an Arab funeral procession. This is the truth. The unelaborate group of three male mourners carried their dead friend (dead for a matter of hours) hoisted high on a board, uncovered, the head facing Mecca. With careful haste, paying us no heed, they dug a deep hole into which they placed the body, upright, as is the custom, and left. . . We left too, returning to the house to play the Fauré *Requiem*. It was early evening and drizzling slightly, though the sun still shown. Then there appeared the most perfect rainbow we had ever seen: one of its feet was a thousand miles south in the Congo somewhere— but the other foot was firmly planted in glimmering glory among the green roofs of Moulay Abdallah, which is the location of all the whorehouses in Fez.

In a flurry of *arrivisme* one year ago—during my initial enthusiasm with this continent of Africa—I mailed to Gide (whom I'd never met) an envelope containing birthday greetings, a song, and an equivocal snapshot of myself. He immediately answered from Paris as follows:

André Gide
I bis, rue Vaneau
Paris—7°   *Le 24 Décembre 49.*

Mon cher Ned Rorem,
   Combien je vous envie: j'ai gardé si bon souvenir de Fez! Un des séjours les plus agréables que j'y ai fait, c'était avec un jeune ami, Robert Lévesque, lequel vient d'être nommé professeur au lycée de Fez; cela doit suffire comme adresse. Je pense que vous auriez probablement, vous et lui, un certain plaisir à vous recontrer.
   Merci pour le ALLELUIA. Trop fatigué pour vous en écrire plus long. Je n'ai de force que pour vous serrer la main en pensée, bien cordialement.

                               André Gide

   Naturally I looked up Lévesque, whom I didn't take to at first: he may have been *jeune* to Gide, but to me he was forty, and his sexual obsession was embarrassing. Moreover, he talked even to his peers as to illiterate children, illiterate children being his sole preoccupation both professionally (at the *lycée*) and socially (when, as always, on the make). But he was, and is, the best Fez had to offer intellectually, and we ultimately became friends. (North Africa, let it be said, is more "cultured" than France: the tackiest *colon,* being out of the swim, feels duty-bound to attend all artistic functions—and there are many, mostly high class, which come touring from Brussels to these provinces. But I've also seen Wilde's *Salomé* performed by natives in Arabic.) Contrary to most here, Lévesque's clean intelligence stems from inside; when he can be diverted from *his* subject, he can be diverting indeed. It is clear that his relationship to Gide (as described in the latter's journal, as well as by himself) was less one of literary colleague than of companion in crime, even of *maquereau.* But his honest satyr's grin permits us to forgive him everything.

❦

The knuckles of my hand and my arm up to the elbow are shot with pains from working so much in the composer's cramped position. But never have I been so pleased with my own music: I have a recognizable style. At the moment I am polishing and copying the chorale pieces I wrote last month at Marie Laure's. Am also writing three "medieval" songs to be sung by Gordon Heath; they are in the manner of Folksong. Folksong (that is to say, Art "in the rough") has never interested me; I have always thought it a medium for unmusical Communists. I remember as an adolescent in Chicago I was vaguely acquainted with some now-vanished members of the YCL. They would sit around for hours listening to records of Burl Ives or Richard Dyer Bennett, expiring in joy at what they thought was the "true expression." This is because folk music has appeal through association: by way of the words. Real music has no fixed associations. The artist *cannot* be concerned with politics, for a regime may change each year, but a work of art remains. I prefer folk music as rewritten by, say, Roy Harris than in its original form. Art is made by tricks played in memory, and our souvenir of an experience is never exact. Art is the artifice of recollection. . .

In Fez, just outside of the great purple gate of Bou-Jeloud, there is a slaughterhouse. At night one can crouch beside the low windows, and through the grating see the death of camels. These prehistoric monsters, chewing their cud with terror in the reddish gloom, wait in line for their individual massacre. And all around the soggy smell of death. An Arab workman fells the beast with a single blow on the temple, after which comes the astonishing echo of a shriek. . . In Paris last winter it was my misfortune to witness a criminal masterpiece in the form of a documentary called *Le Sang des Bêtes.* It is a series of episodes taken in a French *abattoir,* showing how domestic animals are killed. The film was cruel because the animals are presented as human (close-ups of frightened eyes, bleating, helplessness, mass hysteria, etc.), and because the background music was of a young girl's voice singing nursery tunes.

Three days ago Monsieur Bogeart, Guy's medical assistant here, accidentally swallowed some leeches with a scoop of well-water. They have lodged at the back of his throat just out of reach, and are getting regularly larger. Bogeart, normally of flaming complexion, has grown quite white. Perhaps for the moment this is good for his health as he is a fat man. But he begins to have trouble breathing. The leeches may grow so big as to burst, which would be one solution (he spits blood already); or they may descend to his stomach and die of acid mixtures. But they may also remain where they are (unobtainable save by instruments most obscene), necessitating the continuation of nicotine injections in his throat. This puts the creatures to sleep with the hope they'll loose hold, but it also makes poor Monsieur Bogeart so drowsy that if the leeches don't soon expire he's likely to. Meanwhile he keeps on with his daily routine, which was always quite dull, the only change being that he no longer takes wine or salad oil.

There is a pastry shop in Tangier without equal in the world. It's on the hill across from the French Embassy, and instead of a door, it has a thousand threads of jangly beads to keep the flies out (or in). This makes it very like the movies, and the delights within are similarly fantastic. My favorite is the *tarte aux poires,* a wee individual pie all gushing with golden pears and slightly colored with random cherries; the flakey crust is even lovelier than *Good Housekeeping* advertisements. Guy likes better the devil's food cakelets stuffed with cream swirls, because whipped cream is more of a delicacy for the French than for us. Whereas Themistocles Hoetis prefers a sort of small mountain of wafers topped with a strewing of green coconut (a bit too dry for my taste) about which he makes the staggeringly original observation that it's like Coca-Cola: the more you partake the more you desire. Paul Bowles always chooses an almond paste with squirts of gray sugar. But there are all manner of alternate goodies stacked high on the chromium table; Flaubert would have turned pale at the extravagance of mixtures: every combination of fruit and dough known to man is arranged in a dump from which one selects, piling plates high, and heading for one of the lacy tables (probably already occupied by a Spanish family, dogs and grand-parents included). Needless to say we accompany our confection with either a *glace pistache* or a *café liègeois* or both, and then careen into the sunlight feeling sick but full of praise. It was in this establishment that Truman Capote performed a dance last week, but the customers were all too glutted to change expression.

Peach Surprise. When I'm on the wagon (it's classical) I'm so hysterically fond of desserts I can't enjoy the first helping for thinking of the second.

The weather is ferociously hot (or rather, passively hot) which makes one feel a mist, though the sky is clear. This week is the height of Ramadon, the Mohammedan lent; everyone fasts by day, and rejoices by night; there is no sleep.

Last night there was an accident on the route to Taza. A passenger bus collided with a truck, and twenty Arabs were burned to death in the trap (*carbonisés* as the French papers say). We got there around nine-thirty. The car was on its side which increased its size. A desert road, deserted. Crickets chirped. There was still a thickish smoldering. Nothing recognizable: pieces of chest, steaming jawbones, a foot—all nearly powdered. On removing a burnt jacket the flesh too came off. The smoke still twists around the flashlights which move here and there.

Dream: Standing in a street I don't know in Tangier with Paul Bowles, we are aware that "bull-training" is going on over there in a field behind that building. A tree one hundred feet high looms above the building, and gradually we see a bull—a great black bull—moving slowly through the upper branches. He is, as it were, guided from the ground by radar, and (like some cats) can climb but not descend. Carefully he steps among the highest twigs, chooses a final one into space, treads it like a pirate's plank, and falls with a crash to the earth from which rises an ugly pink dust of dying. Loud cheers.

France, Edith Piaf is your great lady. She knows the secret of popular song (the secret Bernhardt knew so well) which is expressivity through banality, the secret of knowing what must be added where. This formula can apply only to "popular" artists: they interpret mediocre works by completing them. Jennie Tourel, on the other hand, is a great lady because she adds nothing. One does not add to art.

Edith Piaf who—with the now-immortal Cerdan—is France's idol, has for me too almost replaced Billie Holiday. I cannot forget how, rue de la Harpe and later at the Hôtel du Bon La Fontaine, we would sit for hours on end drinking wine and listening again and again to those two records ("Un homme comme les Autres," "Je m'en fous pas mal") sung by this brave unnoticeable, tiny, rigid woman, tears streaming down our faces, knowing that we ourselves were in her mouth, a mouth howling the most brazen clichés.

Two years ago I wrote my parents who were worried about how much money to send: "You have given birth to an exceptional child; you must therefore expect exceptional behavior from him." I, in turn, was given an exceptional family who have always made every effort to understand and help.

Morocco is no land of monuments like Italy, it *is* a monument—like America. Nevertheless Rabat contains a muscum (clean, free, silent, neat) with many Roman statues and a few living customers. Among the latter I saw a Berber boy with a face handsome enough to complete the torso he gazed upon. (Or rather, the torso deserved his breathing head.) Beauty shocks, hurts, and forces; the beautifully living countenance (of stupidity even) surpasses those ages of art it inspires.

The paper today tells us that Louis Jouvet and Arthur Schnabel are dead. With Gide, Koussevitzky, and Schoenberg, that makes five who have died these past months. As an adolescent it seemed it was only my young friends who were constantly dying, but that the old people lived on and on, ever more fixed and legendary. This impression is rather true, as I was an adolescent during the war years. I was too young to remember when most of my old relatives died, but between my seventeenth and twenty-first year a series of my dearest contemporaries died; Georg Redlich (23), of an auto accident which deformed him beyond recognition; Don Dalton (24), instantly decapitated by walking into a propeller; Myra Itkonen (24 and a beautiful girl) of a broken back; Lorin Smith (33), his head crushed by a chain as he walked along a California dock; Janet Fairbank (44), finally succumbed to Hodgkin's disease (her arms always black and yellow from injections); unhappy Allela Cornell (30), of suicide by swallowing sulphuric acid. . . Who remembers them? It is to them that I dedicate my series of choral songs *From an Unknown Past. . .*

In Chaucer's day the verb "to die" was synonymous with the verb "to come" ("to have an orgasm").

I have been reading Guy's medical books again, this time a chapter called "De la Mort Apparente." I liked the story of Cardinal Donnet about a young Bordeaux priest in 1826. During his sermon the priest had an attack and fell upon the floor. Pronounced dead by a doctor, his funeral preparations were begun. He was in his coffin, the *De Profundis* was sounding, the earth was falling upon him, when all of the sudden a loud knocking was heard coming from inside the wooden box. The box was opened and the young priest rose up. He had not been dead, but had, in fact, been perfectly conscious and heard the funeral arrangements around him from the voices of friends. He had simply been unable to move or speak. At the end, by a superhuman effort, he managed to make himself audible from the coffin and was liberated.

This is a true medical story to show that death must be certified before burial. For it seems that the human body—hardly breathing in the unconscious state—can live underground for extended periods.

And Guy tells me that at the war's end, when certain of his French friends were freed from Dachau, they strung up their guard by the feet, head down, cut open his neck like a pig, caught the blood in a pail and threw it into his face.

❧

Murder. These two hard syllables have always held a fascination. For several years I have kept a scrapbook of clippings of criminals, or at least people who look criminally interesting (for a criminal is a creator gone wrong, unless perhaps the converse is true): Proust on his deathbed; Edith Sitwell on hers (as seen by Cecil Beaton); the young killer Heirens of Chicago; Paul Klee; Ernst Bloch; the English boy who can't stop hiccuping; Kokoshka; the faces of anonymous athletes; pictures, in other words, of people who attract and revolt me as in the Xondi test. When I was younger I was scared by my loss of conversation at a party; that is still why I drink; though I find that if I begin discussing crime everyone becomes interested. Perhaps I am wrong, but I do not feel this is affectation simply by the fact that when reading of Damien's death (in the book on Sade) I vomited. I can't like the reality of violent cruelty.

I loathe every sort of competition (Quaker?).

The newsreels have shown a new endeavor of a boy going over Niagara Falls in a barrel. He, also, failed. At the news of his death his brother stated that he (the brother) planned to renew the attempt and felt convinced that *he* would succeed. I think this could only have happened in America. For us, any form of failure is a disgrace whether it is concerned with defying Niagara Falls in a barrel, or an indifferent public reaction to a new symphony. We seldom take leisure with a clear conscience; we must try and try again until success comes. If it doesn't come, at least we can say we have died trying. The French have three times as many holidays as Americans, a three-day weekend and a two-hour lunch period. They take their religion seriously (and seldom think about it). The average American works hard at a job he detests and thereby feels that his period of *fun* has been honestly earned. But look at all the weird and useless things we have built. Why? Is it to show our European cousins that we too know how? I believe that we are living to enjoy ourselves and not to be strained and unhappy like Hitler (who nevertheless seems to have been the model leader toward which every young boy is striving). Yet America has the greatest culture of today: our manner is our style and blood.

On the beach earlier this month, discussing certain friends who are addicted to drugs, Jacques Février said, "Oh, to think what they could have done if they hadn't started taking dope; how the talent deteriorates!" But is it not just *because* they were the kind of people who desired to take drugs that they were able to do the wonderful things they've done? We are what we are and because of it we do what we do.

Finished *La Porte étroite* which I read without pleasure, interest, or emotion. Was I afraid of it? of finding myself in it (as we do in all strong works) as a Protestant? I want so to be pagan, yet I know I never shall be. Nevertheless, the last twenty pages moved me despite myself, especially these words on the funeral of Alissa in the letter from Juliette to Jérôme: "They were not the only ones to follow the bier. Some patients from the sanatorium had wanted to attend the ceremony, and to accompany the corpse to the cemetery. . ." I am always touched by this generous boredom in the old, who, deep down, are glad it's not *they* who died.

Also, in Alissa's journal: "Sadness is a state of sin. . . Sadness is a complication. I never tried to analyze my happiness." And: "All of a sudden, he asked me if I believed in an afterlife. 'But, Jérôme,' I cried out immediately, 'for me, it's more than a hope: it's a certainty. . .'

"And suddenly it seemed that all my faith had poured itself into that cry." (*"Et brusquement il m'a semblé que toute ma foi s'était comme vidée dans ce cri."*)

Did Gide mean her faith had left her? Then: "The path which you teach us, Lord, is a narrow path, too narrow to walk two abreast."

Three minutes after putting down this book, I made love with abandon. Now I am sorry, as it seems an insult to everybody.

❦

The heat is relentless and I have never felt so constantly exhausted. Yesterday, finally, Guy decided to give me again some of the horse-blood capsules I took last spring. The result was a frightful attack of sneezing and itching and a paralyzing stomach-ache which lasted for hours. In analyzing this, it appears that I have always been allergic to everything concerning horses. The only time I ever rode (summer 1935 at Yellowstone Park) my eyes became swollen slits, I sneezed incessantly, my hands bled. As a child my inoculations for diphtheria (a horse serum) put me to bed with fever. Later in Paris, on rue de la Harpe, when Xénia and Jean-Claude in their luxuriant poverty used to have feasts of horse steak, the very smell of the meat cooking would give me fainting fits. . . It's amusing to think that this allergy might be psychosomatic, and yet I feel so friendly towards horses, especially when reading Swift's "Voyage to the Country of the Houyhnhyms."

❦

One thing that amused me about Rome last summer was the intense sexuality everywhere. It seems the Italians (who love it any old time or place) wait especially for the Holy Year to come around every quarter of a century. This spells special fun. For instance, before going into St. Peter's for the first time, we stopped to get our pilgrims' tickets stamped in a classy kiosk just made for that purpose. The agent of information took me for French as I was with Guy. *"Tenez! Je vais vous donner cette médaille gratuitement (bénie par le pape, bien entendu!) parce que je sais que vous êtes croyant. Vous en avez l'air,"* said he, pinning the token onto my shirt with clumsy leisure, tickling my chest the while with his little finger. *"Et vous pouvez revenir n'importe quand; j'y serai toujours à votre disposition! Aimez-vous Rome?"* he rippled in his Italian accent, which makes it hard to understand (the Spanish speak better French, I don't know why). . . . *"Le bedeau de la cathédrale de Sienne nous a chatouillé les fesses,"* and winked deliciously as he uncovered the wonderful parquet, but he took a tip all the same. . . They are far from vicarious, so the onanism rate is doubtless low; they've lost none of Nero's giddy abandon. The brothels were closed for Holy Year. *Quel coup!* On every corner are such inexpensive temptations (not to mention the pettiest trickeries) that the year seems holy only to the pope and some of his foreign friends. For the others it's a quarter-century carnival. Sam Barber likes the story of a friend, who, seeking an uncontaminated native, went far away to a mountain village near the Swiss border. For reasons unnecessary to relate, he found himself in a sleeping bag with the blacksmith's child. "Oh, I don't mind," said the blacksmith's child, "as long as you give me two hundred lira."

The Jews here paint their houses blue. That color repels flies. The Moslems cut off their nose to spite their face, and refuse to paint *their* houses blue.

Three Beautiful Birds of Paradise. Why do I retch reading Falla's interview on advice to young composers (or any other master's council, for that matter)? They all say the same thing: don't hurry to publish, work slowly, reflect. Then they all cite Ravel, who would pause a year between completion and presentation; and they all mention their "private" discovery which is inevitably that most priceless of priceless things, *Trois beaux oiseaux du Paradis.* I first heard it at age sixteen. Looking for a practice room (one of Northwestern's gray, brothel-like cubicles), I became aware of magic from behind a door. I had to go in. There sat a soprano, deciphering at the keyboard, squeaking prettily. "But what *is* it?" "Why it's from Ravel's *Trois Chansons* and all the mezzos in school are auditioning tomorrow for the solo in the second one." So we went through it together—and I was floored! This lady, pale and plain, a Public School Music Major on the verge of donating uninspired instruction to untalented children (the desire to teach is itself vain, destructive, indicative of uncreation)—what right *she* to this wonder! I later stole a library copy and have been on my knees ever since (take that as you will); it was mine. Such moments that break the heart also open the ears; how could I not have dreamed of France! People don't think like this anymore; or if they try, they don't succeed. I won't believe that Ravel toiled to make *that* one come out: it just was, born from the words. Perhaps I shall make my new song "Philomel" into a chorus with *soli*—it could be done in one *coup* (and if I do, it will be better work than a slave's). He alone could make any noise he wished, and at the same time worth listening to, rehearing indefinitely. Now we're going swimming.

At 4 A.M. we all went to swim at Sidi Hrasem. Yesterday's unprecedented rain made the *piscine* overflow with warmth reflecting the post-card violet of the palm leaves. It's not easy to bribe the guardian to let you enter: a week ago a woman was murdered in the pool and parts of her are still floating around.

It's cheaper and quicker than divorce which, however, is not difficult with Moslems.

There is a new insane-asylum in Fez; the old one's abolished. The old one was more savage than Hogarth, with the moaning Arabs, already centuries away from our world, lying year after year in their iron collars and chains, in horse stalls crusty with excrement and pails brimming with abominations. The asylum of Tangier is still like this. Guy tells me that the new institutions are built just for outer show but the patients still bang their heads against the wall. To approach the asylum of Marrakech by car, is to approach a motionless wind: a deadly wail comes from that building for twenty-four hours at a stretch, then fades sickeningly as the car recedes. . . As a child I remember the kitchen of the "violent ward" in Yankton, South· Dakota: grayish mashed potatoes in iron vats like those filled with boiling lead in medieval torture chambers. . . The grammar-school language for mental hospital: booby hatch, loony bin, nuthouse, bughouse, laughing factory, etc. How far from the troubling poetry of Yeats about the insane ("Sweet Dancer," for instance).

To get to the Mérinèdes roadhouse from Fez proper you take the road that leads out of the new town past Avenue de France, but instead of going into the civil prison (across from which we live) you turn right on the road which surrounds the town and also leads to the Palais Jamai. You pass the graveyard—which is white and decorative, but foul-smelling (because Moslems are buried upright, and at night hyenas come to gnaw their skulls)— and pass also a little annex city where people live like cave dwellers. In five minutes you arrive at the highest point of the foothills by which Fez is tightly closed in. There, someone has built a café and called it Les Mérinèdes; you could recognize it with your eyes closed by the smell of mint tea and *kif*. The latter is indistinguishable from marijuana and its odor makes me slightly sick. Guy drinks *Oulmès* and I drink *Jus d'or,* local soft drinks from which we never switch. The view is of course frightfully exciting—especially at night—and not unlike the approach to Mexico City via the mountains south. Every house in old Fez is visible as in a child's garden or the *hameau* at Versailles (or Florence, except that in Florence all the roofs are reddish, while those here are of a dull religious jade). Lights and noises from afar are, I suppose, about the most pregnant impetus which exists to sentimental situations. And one can see over the glittering valley to the mountain on a level with you. But it has no cozy den for drinking *Jus d'or*. Here in our Café des Mérinèdes we sit in deck-chairs poised like rabbits above a sheer drop of a thistley hundred feet (best stick to *Jus d'or*). There are no other European clients, only the Arab *patron* and his friends, all high as kites on their hashish that is always consumed with mint tea (which, on the other hand, smells divine). There's said to be an art to its making, though I can't see why: It's tea in a pot with chunks of raw sugar and clear mint in dewy broken bunches stuffed to the brim. Drunk in steaming glasses—which makes it as irritating as *café-filtre*—it is as characteristic as the *kif* which always accompanies it. (Is that why our slang for marijuana is "tea"? Personally I prefer alcohol, not liking to be consecutively aware of my follies as they occur.) This is no place for rendezvous; they take place along the dark river which dissects the the town: a hotbed of hot people who have no beds. I have cut all my hair off and look like a fool or a chicken. My head is velvety with nothing but glinty traces of the *eau oxygenée* put there months ago.

Admitting to be a fool doesn't keep one from being a fool. The public is lazy, likes only lies. From the minute they sense the truth they lose interest.

A few moments ago, as I was sitting on the toilet reading
Giraudoux, a big insect flew in the window. It looked like a
wingèd scorpion with a Frankenstein head. It hovered hypnotized, stared at me, quivered a full minute, and then flew off
again. But I could do nothing more.

Part 4

Paris:

September - December, 1951

Back in Paris for four days. . . Rain. . . And an atrocious welcome: we had drunk a lot of brandy on the airplane from
Marseilles and landed tired in Paris at midnight. Then of course
I stayed out most of the night drinking with forgotten friends.
Returning home, I was attacked on the Place St. Michel by a
Senegalese—who blackened my lovely left eye, stole my passport,
boat ticket to America, two hundred dollars in traveler's checks,
and a pair of glasses. A gratuitous crime, since none of these
objects can be of use to the robber; yet I am left without a
country. I'm broken by this, especially since I have always felt
invulnerable, yet calamity befalls me every third week. I have
been spending my first days here then, looking in the mirror at
the black eye on this face which, Julien says, in a few years no
one will notice any longer in the street, and by that signal I
shall know that I have gotten old.

My hotel—the Bisson—is between the Pont Neuf and Pont
St. Michel. For the moment I have an expensive room which
looks onto the Seine, and across the river is the police station,
Quai des Orfèvres, where two years ago I was held for a night
after a raid on a St. Germain bar. Upon the river, between the
police and my window, there is nothing but rain and rain and
rain. Leaves are turning color, and today is the first of fall.

At the beginning of the month, after my return from Morocco,
Marie Laure took me to Venice for Charles Bestigui's ball, and

for the première of *The Rake's Progress* (interchangeable functions, you might say). The housing shortage was so crucial that we shared a room at the Danieli with Christian Mégret sleeping in the bathtub. I was the youngest and worst-dressed at the Palazzo Labia, from where I returned at eleven next morning to find this letter on my pillow:

Darling,
I was feeling so tired that I thought it better to go home: inferring that you were all right with Tony or Christian. I am frantic with anxiety—got into your bed all morning. Bless you. I love you truly.

Marie Laure

Am I wrong? Do I "use" people? Was Venice cursed? Has Marie Laure (with tears and coiffure trailing over her evening gown in the noon of St. Mark's, before her own daughter and all of society) simply a taste for scandal? Is it too soon to know?

❦

It is more difficult to write words on one's family than on any other subject. Probably if I were able to elucidate certain acts and sensations performed and experienced as regards my parents and sister (which I shall never have the courage to do, even after their deaths), then I would no longer feel the crushing necessity to be an artist.

❦

The only reason I don't commit suicide is because I'm afraid to be alone. And yet, being among people, I am distant from them all. Really I should be done away with, being a two-headed monster.

❦

Talked for an hour with Dora Maar who, for four years, did not drink a drop, even of wine. Four months is as big an oath as

I can take, and I swear here not to drink at all until February (at which time some of the habit will be lost).

I'm not working well either: the desire is terribly there, but my imagination simply cannot focus on the ballet I'm supposed to be writing. This imagination vanished with the robbery in the solitude of Paris. Besides, I cannot think except for the human voice.

My room has been changed. Now I am high up, looking onto a court and Latin Quarter roofs. A piano and a bathtub. Everyone is so very good to me (but where is the *difference* between any two people?). I miss Guy.

Yet when I go through periods of abstinence—although I am smug in my buoyancy—I feel always in a state of *not being drunk*. This is an artificial state, but it can hardly be said to be harmful.

> *Belles journées, souris du temps,*
> *Vous rongez peu à peu ma vie.*
> *Dieu! Je vais avoir vingt-huit ans*
> *Et mal vécus, à mon avis.*
> —APOLLINAIRE, La Souris

Today is my birthday. (This is not true; I will not be twenty-eight until after tomorrow. But today I have birthday thoughts, and anyway have been feeling twenty-eight for some time.) October 23rd was also Franz Liszt's birthday, and Sarah Bernhardt's. And 1923 when I was born, was the year of Sarah's death. Also Fauré's. Did a wand touch me at birth, instilling me with the living souls of these people? Certainly all my music is slow like Fauré's (his fast music is really slow music played fast). Certainly I constantly play-act like Sarah; except that this "acting," being a part of me, is no longer acting. . . Twenty-eight years! But I stopped learning at twenty-five. And I shall spend from now till fifty either trying to forget what I have found out, or attempting to adapt it all into something nice and selfish and profitable. For nothing seems new anymore. If I went to China I would feel I had seen it before. . . But like any child I know the world was made for me; I am incapable of foreseeing a gloomy future.

Her husband Charles being away, Marie Laure took me and Jerry Robbins to his house for the weekend, the former Palais de Pompadour in Fontainebleau. Leaves had fallen and rotted, the corridors were icy, every gorgeous room had fires like the one shining from Googie Withers' mirror in *Dead of Night*. By Saturday Jerry and I were so uneasy from Dominguez' habitual pranks, from our hostess' weird indulgence, from the atmosphere in general, that we decided to play a joke. As we dressed in our wing for the evening meal we invented this romance to relate while dining: "We were dressing when there was a knock. At the door stood a woman in filmy black, coiffed in eighteenth-century style, and with tears on her cheeks. She beckoned, and as we approached she turned, floated down the hall, entered a guest room, and closed the door. We followed—but found only an empty parlor except for a pool of tears on the rug.". . . While dining I began to relate: "We were dressing, when a woman in tears appeared at the door—" Marie Laure interrupted: "Was she coiffed in eighteenth-century style and dressed in filmy black?" We babbled: "Yes." "Well, of course! She's the ghost of Charles' ancestor, la Comtesse de ——, who used to inhabit your wing."

My dream life being of considerably more interest than my real one, I see no reason for not staying in bed twenty-four hours a day. Especially during this thick French bleak gray drunk season one feels like crawling back toward the *"bon grand fond malampia"*! Anyhow, who's to say that our waking life might not be the one of dreams, and contrariwise?

Last night I walked alone all over Paris searching and searching for miles on end. Toward two in the morning, tumbling with fatigue down one of those empty lanes between the Luxembourg and the boulevard St. Germain, I suddenly heard the hollow tones of wooden-heeled footsteps approaching from far behind. I smiled to myself, slowed my pace, the feet came nearer, growing louder, swifter. When they were nearly upon me I shivered and was thrilled. Then the steps passed me—but I saw no one. The regular clack of the feet walking before me grew fainter, farther away, turned a corner and disappeared. But I hadn't seen a soul. . . I went to bed and had this dream. I was escaping in a canoe down a deep jungle river, but the travel was slow as trees hung low at every point. Surly savages emerged and disappeared on the night land. While paddling I looked down and saw far below the surface two dismembered feet, dead and luminous, walking with a terrifying slowness, like floating plants. I was to be likewise cut apart if my flight were unsuccessful.

Today lunch with Balthus at the Catalan and afterwards a visit to his very messy studio (it resembles what must have been the interior of the Collier brothers' home) in the adorable Cour de Rohan just off the rue Jardinier. Balthus is working on a most frightening oil. The canvas is enormous, four yards wide, and high as the ceiling. On this are nothing but two curious girls:

one, a naked dead doll in false light stretched on a couch awaiting love; the other, a vital little idiot sister in a green sweater opening the curtain and exposing her rival to the real light of the sun. There is also a vase and cat. All this in colors hitherto uninvented. . . I had to shiver! Poor great Balthus: so Jewish and sorry for himself; so rich, so poor.

Later in the day I went to see Bernac. Who could be more contrary to Balthus? which doesn't keep him from being just about as sad. Overly neat, overly tolerant (to me tolerance means getting old). He feels nobody loves him, and this may be true, though he is one of our master singers.

But I loathe more and more discussing music in any form or shape. We spend most of our lives repeating ourselves. To say I want to stay home doesn't prevent me from going out and repeating myself. I loathe concerts, but this didn't prevent me from going tonight to be bored by Igor Markevitch. What is sadder than a half-filled concert hall? Nothing. Backstage Igor is sad and cold (*bien qu'il m'ait tutoyé pour la première fois*), Boulanger is icy, Marcelle de Manziarley frigid, Poulenc chilled in a box with his peculiar niece, everyone is glacial and lacking in glamor. Concerts need glamor.

This was my Thursday, omitting important things like street-walking.

Paris today is a city asleep. And snoring loudly.

What I have longed for most during these awful days has not been my forgotten music, but the snow in New York. I should like to sit and drink rye in the Café Royale on Second Avenue once again and watch the snow falling slowly outdoors onto that brightly lighted Jewish theater. And as I drink to think about how everybody loves me.

The more I think of my short but not short enough conversation with Souvchinsky, the more my blood boils. He simply cannot be talked to (a woman I would forgive, a man should know better). He always chooses the wrong time to express himself, as at a party, where people need only say things they don't care about. How am I to answer when he asks, "Don't you think that Boulez' is the only music today? That he is taking the only possible path?" Of course I don't think so; I am a composer too and Boulez' path isn't mine. What's more, Boulez will not attain the nonexpressive element he seeks because his "system" has as origin *le dodécaphonisme*, inherently the most expressive of musical devices. . . Nevertheless I was disconcerted.

I am content with my work, the *Cycle of Holy Songs* and the ballet for Jerry. There is nothing on earth of which I'm not capable except experimentation. Because I am an American Protestant. How I love the French! And I love Americans too for their youthful sweetness in apologizing for every daily action.

1 A.M. Almost I am afraid to write here tonight for fear that clarifications may make me burst into tears, knowing my whole life has been only an expedition of waiting. Seven days of chaos began with my return from Denmark. How could I dare transfer my reactions to this trip? How dare look back upon these seven days since? the worst nightmare of any all interspersed and oozing with heavy sick and juicy dreams, more crazy and real than life.

Yesterday Marie Laure gave a lunch to which she had the bad sense (or unconscious cruelty) to invite me as spectator. Because—although I'd known each of the guests before—all of them were old friends from the last generation, and all were painters. And painters with musicians have nothing in common (as everyone knows: it's all been explained before). But let me describe them as freaks:

Léonor Fini has a mysterious round hat made from a pea-green furry substance, and a coat to match. This is how she is naked when coming out from behind her famous masks; with a laugh of masculine assurance she echoes all other sounds in the room which reach her, only to have them bounce off again from her green hat. She is like her own picture without enough power for real cruelty or pathos. I tell her, "You haven't the right to draw men who love, because you are a woman and if you go any farther you'll reach a dangerous land where you're not wanted and be pushed from a cliff breaking your thick neck. Since a woman's hand that desires to depict a man's domain is, by nature, incapable of making the excitement it seeks, it can only make embarrassment." She laughs again and says, "I'd like to make you cry." She couldn't though; I just burn with anger. But of course, being me, I say nothing.

We all know Dali. I'll just mention that if he were of my métier and generation I would spit in his face. It's hideous to see humanity leave a man as he grows progressively more famous. Screaming on sex is funny, but one cannot joke about war in parlor conversation. He had said, "We need more wars, but shorter ones." Where will *he* be? It's *I* who will die a painful death. What has he done that approaches *Guernica*? I am ashamed to be in a room with Dali, his mustache, his cane; I blush that my parents should discover I have known him; my mother, who has devoted her life to peace.

Now I wish just for knowledge of the simplicity of love-making. Just to drink every night with beloved Heddy de Ré (who knows how), or write little operas with gentle Elliott Stein (who can be funny), or to cry with bewitching Marie Laure (who has found out how to read books). Yet I know that I will never know that love-making is a thing of nature.

11:30 A.M. It's now been fourteen days since I've had a drop. This period on the wagon has been more necessary than any of the others, since finally my health seemed corroded. But I only emerge into the raw light of great doctor bills, absence of love, incapacity for work. I prefer the sensation of being drowned. More and more I appear to be getting *insaisissable*, even to myself; when I stand apart I see my body moving about the city like a self-denying marionette. To look back on this two week orgy of sterile sobriety and realize that in any case I was doing the same things as when I'm drunk (only less blurred), for instance, being in that place full of semifemale impersonators, rue de Bourgogne, where a wiry queen with incredible hair, who looks like a cross between Jean Harlow and Harpo Marx, is weeping on the bar; or the Club de Paris (there is a pianist in similar clubs all over the world—in St. Louis or Hong Kong— who plays the same tunes in the same way, without rhythm, without energy, like rubber for the same pallid withering chromium clientele, which chatters and never gets drunk): it's the not being alone—or, if I find myself alone, I become frightened and can think of nothing to say to myself. So I see hundreds of people, bad or indifferent, and can't tell one from another—and can't wish to work. Well, then what is the use of being in superlative physical condition if this wonderful instrument of the body can't profit thereby? So Heddy and I have made a date for next Friday to get conscientiously plastered, beginning in the Pont Royal bar. She'll be there before me (as I must come directly from the dentist) with a bottle of olive oil: it seems that if the stomach is lined then the liquor causes no suffering. What good is it to be aware, to see all real things closely or know every muscle of the beings which fly around you in space? It is not for nothing that God has made me nearsighted: I converse with deep-sea animals. *Et le bon Dieu me permet de déconner.*

Mid-afternoon was like night with a fog thick as London, through which came a hard hot red-silver sun absolutely round, looking as though it were the twilight of the world. In this cold soup I walked around to toy stores with Stephen Spender and Peggy Bernier buying gifts—pistols and glass sailors!—for their children (and *he* a pacifist! *We* were never allowed guns). Then we had coffee *aux Deux Maggots,* and Stephen is certainly better in Paris than England (like all the English away from their wives) but depressing all the same, since he would like to save the world, and this is something I generally try not to think about. Also all his tastes have a firm basis in the Germanic and therefore, of course, he doesn't feel for French art, which makes the two of us essentially different. I can't agree with his personal definition, but he says: German art constantly moves, comes toward you and passes like a train; but the whole French aesthetic is based on *cooking* in a series of additions (a pinch of garlic here, some tomato sauce there); that it works fine in painting, but that the music seems to be seen and not heard. . . Of course the curt preciousness of this kind of expression is basically French already, and therefore Stephen's opinion (as long as he uses these words) cannot, for the moment, mean anything.

Encore des séries de bonnes cuites! I thought I'd been able to stop. No, this time I've come home with a deep gash in the forehead and a deep depression. Last night was Cocteau's new *Bacchus,* during which I came close to dying: my green forehead a mass of sweat. I try—but can only remember a sequence of faces.

The *gaffe* I made at Marie Blanche's a few weeks ago was divine! Little François Valéry (son of the late Paul Valéry) was there. And the three of us were chatting about Leonard Bernstein, who had just married and settled in Cuernavaca. Marie Blanche said, "How lovely! What adorable and talented children they'll have!" upon which she reeled across the room, her face smiling and blank, and collapsed into a large armchair. But I replied, "Oh, I don't think so: children of the great are always *cons*!". . . No sooner had this escaped my lips than I realized what I had said. What could I have added to expiate my crime?—that, after all, Paul Valéry was insignificant?

Maggy's marvelous breakfast of long ago: eggs in pepper rings poached in cider and served with Canadian bacon. . .

Livid descriptions of my drunkenness reach me again from all sides: how, once, on a stormy morning in Cherry Grove, I crawled out of the sea and fell into the house of a strange blond girl, saying, "I want to die." This girl, it seems, is now in France and remembered me (like so many others) not as a composer but as a drunk. . .

Lise Deharme's dinner was a catastrophe: Marie Laure, to impress Milhaud (tragic in his silver wheelchair), monopolized the conversation; my forehead began to bleed again and I also broke a vase; Sauguet was his nastiest to everyone; Jacques Perrin was drunk and cruel. The only coherent conversation was devoted to the Cocteau play, and it was sad to see the disappointment of old friends. . . I'm beginning to prefer the eternal night-mares of my sleeping hours to those of waking.

   Christmas night: In a state of complete exhaustion; am losing weight, becoming more and more fragile, frighteningly pale. These days leading toward Christ's rebirth have been scary and surrealistic, beginning with *Les Noces* which always leaves me feeling slight. Then a pointless dinner at Marie Blanche's where I played my *Sicilienne* at two pianos (with Robert V.-L.) and nobody said they liked it because Sauguet hates me on account of Jacques Dupont, and that is Paris society, more babyish and spiteful than in America. During these days Chapeauval committed suicide, and Tom Keogh slit the wrist of his right arm (he's left-handed)—his room was drenched in blood, even the windows. Every painter I've ever known has killed himself at Christmas time, never in summer, always at Christmas. Because when there's no light the painter is lost (he doesn't know how to read), and in December there's little daylight. So he fills himself with alcohol and dies. . .

   Suicides which succeed are, in a sense, failures; one seldom does it to die: the implied blackmail would be worthless without the instigator's enjoyment. No one believes in his death: one attends one's own funeral—as guest, not corpse.

   To sink so low that only rising is conceivable—and then to sink lower!

   New Year's eve was pretty much like this: lunch with Claude Bénédick can be skipped as of no importance; then I changed

money at Julius'; then I went to Milhaud's to finish a nervous
dark afternoon of thaw, and to begin the end of a year. Milhaud
for twenty-five years has lived in a barren apartment on the
Boulevard Clichy looking down into the million wild lights of
Pigalle's merry-go-rounds. He is enormously fat in all parts of his
body (it is said that his sweat glands don't function), and literally
does not walk: his life is spent in a chromium wheelchair. But
his voice is music itself. Being the most significant of *"Les Six,"*
he is less *maître* than any of them: has none of Poulenc's
elegance, Tailleferrc's *bêtise*, Auric's worldliness, Durey's non-
existence, or Honegger's weariness. He loves youth and lives for
music, and when he tells me good things about my work I forget
what anyone else ever said. As with all elderly composers, I felt
a certain sadness come into Milhaud's expression when I entered;
a feeling of disappearance before new growth as if he were saying
to himself: "Soon this boy will be breathing my air."

Coming out onto the always exciting mystery of the Boulevard
Clichy I had difficulty finding a taxi, so I arrived late at the
réveillon of Marie Laure. There was lots of champagne, quarreling, and tears, but no sense of Christmas, though I kept screaming the child Christ was born. I recall that someone described a
Chinese torture, consisting of a rat in a cage, the open side of
which is placed against the buttocks; fire is applied to the other
side of the cage, forcing the rat, in his terror and suffering, to
gnaw his way into the victim's body by way of the rectum. We
all became drunk, and at eleven the florist delivered a practical
joke sent by the Lopez': a life-sized figure made of flowers, which
looked like Frankenstein dressed as a woman. This took three
hours to burn, and expired with hideous fiery twists.

After this, everything crumbles; I remember only Oscar,
Balthus, Etienne P., and Dora, and have a hazy recollection of
receiving the next day Juliet and Man Ray, with Heddy (naked)
in bed beside me, eating sandwiches and saying to the beautiful

Christian Mégret, about me, *"Ne vous en faites pas pour moi; je ne baise jamais mes soeurs!"*

A mouse has just died in my piano. I believe she entered there to give birth, but was killed instead by the hammer strokes.

Then my life is brightened just a bit by the good and delightful libretto that Elliott made for me. It was drawn from Hawthorne's "The Snow Image," but we call it *A Childhood Miracle*.

With reddish-gold brown hair and a wonderful nose, dressed in black shoes and socks, jet-black corduroy jacket and trousers, coal-black jersey shirt with a Byronic collar from Dominique Franz, the wide wine-colored tie of softest velvet (the birthday gift Julius Katchen found in Munich); and the spectacular little bandage on my forehead, which is beginning to bleed again. This is how I appeared at *Bacchus*; and now I blush.

I have a horror of sluggishness, moral or bodily. What have I done since May, 1949? I have composed and orchestrated and beautifully copied in India ink and had performed a symphony, a string quartet, a piano sonata, an opera, a fiddle sonata, a piano concerto, five song cycles, fifty songs, a suite of songs for voice and orchestra, a Design for orchestra, three ballets, and a great deal of choral music and short piano (and miscellaneous) pieces most of which are already published; I have also traveled; given concerts and broadcasts; written three volumes of this journal and three thousand letters; made and lost countless important friends and unimportant ones; written articles; fallen in love three times; exerted my charm and my ugliness to a maximum—

not to mention having gotten dead drunk and recovered at least four hundred times. In other words I have maintained what I consider my duties on Earth, though I nevertheless have a constant guilty conscience for what I consider my laziness. . .

After his little party last Thursday, Virgil tells me that since I am the only "star" representing America in Paris at the moment (that is, the only expatriate composer), it's my responsibility to be well-behaved, and if I can't pay the bills, then not misbehave, but smile politely and go home and work.

Let's develop our faults: they're our true nature.

The alcoholic can stop drinking, and when he does, he has milk, does exercises, sleeps well, goes to movies. He can stop drinking, but only for a while. His abstinence never lasts. There is always the image of a glass waiting; it's the glass that gets impatient, not the drinker. And there is always the startled expression at his new happy body. He says: Why get into good condition if not to break it down again? Is that not why countries arm?

If you drink heavily you find yourself in strange places and never know how you get there (locomotion is not recalled since it's a constant shifting of place, and even a place where you've passed many hours can be obliterated from the memory next day); you find yourself in strange places and in search of something never quite found, since it's more likely to be in the next strange place where you will be drunker. I can remember looking all night for a face seen ten years ago while drunk. We can walk for miles without knowing it. Getting drunk the following day is like wanting to return to bed in order to recapture last night's dream where it left off. The remarkable romances I have had in a stupor, I cannot reduplicate until the next stupor; not because I am too shy, or have misjudged the beauty of a half-forgotten face, but because when I am sober I simply haven't the interest (which could be called a "lack of responsibility") to remain in bars until seven in the morning with other remarkable people who are in the same strange place at seven in the morning. No one has a *sense of order* like an alcoholic on the wagon. But no days are as difficult as those which immediately follow the oath of abstinence (always temporary). The variations are infinite. It is not the physical letdown, lack of ability to work, nor guilt at looking friends in the face, so much as knowing one has renounced a habitual dream of even the goriest myth, the possibility of finding eternal love (usually with some crazy butcher-boy who empties your pockets)—the scary but still magic possibility of waking up, your mouth in shreds and your head in crumbs, staring stupidly at the Tour Eiffel, which looks like a toad with an apothecary's hat.

(Our gifts are not gifts, but paid for terribly.

Part 5
Marrakech, Morocco:
January-February, 1952

Back now in Morocco, wintertime, all feels blue and gold.

But my health all feels worse; if it isn't one thing it's another, and not a moment's peace. The whole side of my face seems paralyzed and my left ear is completely deaf, which makes me live more and more in my own world. I've had to see another doctor here (I left Paris in the middle of dental treatment, teeth still in rags), and he says I'm deaf because I haven't blown my nose in two years; that most creative personalities have ear trouble what's more!

Mother and Father—when Rosemary and I were twelve and eleven—took us to see Nazimova in *Ghosts*. Two women in the row behind whisper: "Shameful! to bring children to such a play"—at which Rosemary turns around and says, "It's people like you that make plays like this necessary!"

I live in Marrakech and do nothing but work. But strangers visit here only to make love, with such single-tracked viciousness that one would think they had no tomorrow. Part of me dies too, as I stand away and watch their insatiable and nervous dance through the square, like ants upon a stove.

If two people find each other in the street, they will be in bed
together an hour later. But how? My desire is to turn and run.
What have they said to each other between street and bed?
That's a magic secret that I've kept myself from knowing. Or, if
I find myself on the way to the bed, I think: it happened this
time, but how will it happen next time? Then—there being no
mystery, and knowing I *could* if I *wanted*—I invent an excuse
and vanish. Because if I found myself in bed, I would want to
reduce myself to that delicious idiocy which is true love. But even
stronger is my fright of losing independence. As I walk I hate
having my arm taken, for my step is my own and nobody else's.
In Latin countries men walk arm-in-arm; Arab men attach them
selves together by crooking their little fingers. I always walk
without physical touch on the left of anyone in order to defend
myself with the right arm. Also I spit a lot to the annoyance of
all friends.

What's weird is to be at home here late at night and all alone
submerged in work of this time, and then to go into the lanes
of Marrakech and find a life of two thousand years ago. To walk
alone at night among the coppersmiths and veiled women selling
bread, the pimps and water-merchants and cobra-charmers, and
the men who sell perfume and the trained pigeons and drums
and flutes all under the shaking night light of tapers burning
and the odor of sweet potatoes. To have left suddenly my quiet
room where I was thinking about twentieth-century music. Then
to dine alone high up on the terrace of the Café de France and
look down upon this squirming square with the wind blowing
through a hundred candles and Arab music. On the other side
of me the restaurant's radio is playing American jazz, and I try
to read *Le Poète Assassiné* as I eat my *fraise melba*. The sound
of the radio makes me remember the windy summers of Chicago
fifteen years ago when we'd go swimming in the lake at mid

night, our wet bodies illuminated by the changing colored lights
of the nearby nightclub which sent the wail of saxophones out
over the water. . .

Marrakech—one of the three hottest cities on earth—is indeed
cool this winter, and the pirate-city of Mogador last Sunday was
like ice.

Mme. P. asked us all to dine with her *à la Maison Arabe, un
restaurant chic (aux salons particuliers) blotti en pleine Médina.*
She's the kind of woman who is only found in colonial towns:
around forty-five, hair bleached pale pink, the withered face of
a monkey, silly and talkative, wealthy (but forced to spend the
winter in Morocco away from her elegant Paris friends because
of her husband's work), crazy about good-looking boys and the
"artistic personality". . . We were six in a private dining room
full of rose and silver cushions like a DeMille harem. I detest
eating with my hands and see no reason for doing so if one is
not the guest of an Arab. Yet this is how we proceeded, even
with a greasy pigeon pie covered with cinnamon. And then
Madame P. asks the question I despise the most (the question
showing that people may love artists, but can't love art): "What
magnificent inspiration you must find in Marrakech, you, a
composer so attuned to beauty! Have you ever written better?". . .
If I *have* written better it's because I've turned my back to the
view. It's hard for people to realize that the artist's inspiration is
always present and all he needs to express it is concentration;
beautiful surroundings are disconcerting. Casanova's marvelous
book was inspired by a prison cell. Ravel pulled down the shade
when he composed, and Wagner closed the palace door. We all
know that the beauty of art is interior, but if the composer
writes what he sees in nature, he'll cultivate nothing more than
Cyril Scott's lotus or MacDowell's wild rose. I've come to this
country to work, not to make love. If I allow myself to go astray

to Tinerhir, which is the garden of Eden, then I am lost. For instance, Sunday we took a long ride—*dans le bled sur la route d'Amismiz*—and this is paradise. Returning at six the sun was setting, and the highway was covered with mad people whose eyes were turned toward the ramparts of Marrakech looking like the wall of China—a belt burning for miles like orange velvet in the dying sun and full of green blood. Nothing could be more silent, so silent I could hear my own circulation like a waterfall of blood in my skull, the noise of blood; and the sadness that always accompanies beauty as we entered the city gate and came to watch the death of the sun in the Place Jemâa-el-Fnâa. Then the lamps begin to go on, one by one, in the square; the fire-eater starts to swallow his torch; under a hundred tents supper is begun.

Because I found it amusing, I sent my parents one of the typical postcards bought in any Moroccan stationery store. It represents two prostitutes in one of the weird whorehouses of the Quartier Réservé. They are naked (except for turkish towels thrust between their legs), heavily made-up, impassive faces, smoking and drinking tea in a Baudelairian décor. Mother was "quite shocked," for, as she wrote, she is "getting older." Her reaction, in turn, shocked me.

Nothing can touch me more than lay-people's love for music. Not those who sit in concert halls, but those who play at home; not those who say, "If only my mother had forced me to practice!" but those who practice anyway. Sometimes in the evening I watch with wonder as Guy practices the piano. He plays badly, but with such devotion (he has a gigantic repertoire by heart) that I realize the greatest pianist in the world could not give him as much joy as his ability to make these sounds himself. So many medical men have a need (not to mention sacred awe) of music; it must be the strain of their profession. Though music in no sense should be a relaxation. (How wrong was Shakespeare's "concord of sweet sounds"! One might just as well say: Painting is a juxtaposition of pretty colors.) It makes me cry with tenderness to realize that Guy has sacrificed voyages to buy the piano with which he has spent months of his life *alone*. Just as a Jew can "spot" another Jew, so can a musician know in a minute whether the person with whom he is talking has a feigned or real love. I've always respected those who say, "Music means nothing to me! I've tried, but it just means nothing." Some are my best friends (perhaps because I'm not afraid of them?). On the other hand I am suspicious of compliments. But those who say, "What chance you have to be among the 'chosen few,' to be able *to create!*"—those are the ones who trouble me, and, without knowing it, make me remorseful for the idiotic life I lead. Yet can any composer truthfully say he's at all times faithful to his work? Our lives are what they are, we live by our responses to other people, *et il n'y a rien à faire*. The true amateur moves the heart, because, for an inch of progress, he has the patience of an ant, yet has no jealousy for those able to travel with ease through the air like angels. I say that the true amateur is the more *complete* and sincere (though I've never thought sincerity a prime quality), whereas I've never known a professional who was not propelled by ambition (which I've never thought a particularly *base* quality). But the amateur has a blind faith in us, a respect for our natural responsibility that we deceive in ways he'll never be aware of. That is why I'm touched by the layman's love: he sees creation as a magic world, and *I* know that it's not.

Evening. Supper at the Ménara. And in all that elegance, what should appear: bedbugs! If there is a bedbug within twenty miles it will find me immediately. (It is like being *en panne* in the desert, far from anywhere, no vegetation, just a hot, empty lunar landscape. Yet a million flies buzz out of nowhere with a savage bite, and groups of Arabs arise like a mirage. Throughout North Africa there are nomads, lone wolves always a bit out of their minds, who, in the wilderness, will lift their *djellabahs* and show you their genitals with a dim smile.) The itching became so atrocious that I had to leave my marvelous soufflé and rush to the washroom, tear off my coat, and discover my arm in shreds. I looked frenetically through my shirtsleeve for the nasty little beast, but of course couldn't find it.

It is often in the chicquest places that bedbugs flourish: the last time for me was in the Parade bar at Tangier, and before that, on the Algerian border two and a half years ago in Oujda's best hotel. Don't tell me! There's nothing I don't know about bedbugs. How my heart leapt to see the delightful pages about this vermin in Casanova's *Histoire de ma Fuite des Prisons de Venise que l'on appelle les Plombs* (an admirable book in any case), which compares with the famous section in *Les Caves du Vatican.*

My first and most harrowing experience with bedbugs was in 1943 when I lived at Xénia's on Delancy Place in Philly. Bedbugs (except in Philadelphia) seldom practice their trade by daylight; and even at night (though you can be rolling in a mass of nervous sweat, a throbbing welt) they are difficult to find when you suddenly turn the light on and search for them in the sheets and woodwork. But those *chez nous* were monsters of shamelessness: all we had to do was sit with our back to the wall in the blaze of noon, and down they would crawl from the moldings, making a "V" like an army of airplanes heading straight for the back of our neck. Then we'd be interrupted in the reading of our Proust (or whatever) by abominable and almost bumpy itching, and realize the bedbugs were out again. But *our* bedbugs were so sluggish and huge, so glutted and thick from our blood, that they could not disappear as we turned around, and we were able to kill them against the wall with the heel of a shoe. *Try* to kill them, I should have said, for their crust is hard as a diamond. But if one of them managed to break, it gave off the sweet nauseating smell of almond extract. They are flat and mean and shiny. A plague: everywhere bedbugs, enormous, even eating each other—not only in the bed and walls, but in books, in the toilet paper, in the piano keys. Our faces were black from sleepless nights, so we called the exterminator. This meant that the apartments above and below had to be vacated for six hours while the exterminator did a spray-job of cyanide. (It turned out later that the people next door hadn't been notified, and their baby was killed by the fumes.) That night after the exterminator's visit, we went to bed with hearts relieved and gay. But two hours later in the black, oh God! the itching began anew, simultaneously with an air-raid siren which meant lights out. But we switched on the light—doped with fatigue and despair—to see the bed aswarm with escaping bedbugs like a hundred maddened crocodiles fighting frantically in a small pool of boiling water. We were consequently fined by the air-raid warden, but as he happened to be Roy, the alcoholic from upstairs, he forgot about it.

When I moved to my little apartment on New York's 285 West 12th Street in 1944, Noel Sokoloff (who, two years before had taken it from Norman Dello Joio, and now was giving it to me) said, "Just remember this: the fireplace doesn't work. It looks quite capable, but it's a 'front'; it would have cost six hundred dollars to make an opening flue into the chimney." That night I came home drunk, and the sodden bedbugs (for Noel had hitherto offered them nothing: they only like certain skin) were wild with joy at my young flesh, and began gnawing immediately. I couldn't stand it; I took my Christmas tree, thrust it into the fireplace and started it flaming, hoping thus (by the drunken reasoning I'd already been using five years) to suffocate the tiny cannibals. And the fire burned wonderfully. Now it seems my chimney let out directly into the apartment above, from which, ten minutes later, a young couple came flying down, their faces black from soot, screaming.

"The baby! Our baby is dying from the smoke!" (another baby!), and we threw a bucket of water onto the Christmas tree—which caused such an additional density of smoke that the fire department arrived. I explained that it was the bedbugs. (I had never lived alone before.) Everyone went back to bed, but I went out again into the night of Village bars (probably the San Remo) and when I finally returned I was not alone. I recall that my companion smelled most unpleasant—so unpleasant, in fact, as to have disgusted the bedbugs and sent them all away. Because the next day they seemed to be quite gone, and I never had contact with another one there, though I lived on in that room for five years.

Not a word from Jerry since the two long letters just after he left Paris in October. Perhaps because of this silence which I'm almost used to, he now seems the only person I'd like to hear from. It's now obvious that our ballet won't be done, at least not this season, and I can't help but think he's embarrassed to write because of his disappointment in the score. (Today, in looking over the music, I too find it forced and hasty and without great interest except for the Waltz already used in *Mélos*.) I believe, too, that Jerry feels my interest in him is "professional"—he being abnormally suspicious—and this hurts. (I'm the opposite: I feel that everyone likes me "for myself alone." Yet, strangely, those who have been the most helpful professionally are editors and performers who've never met me.) I could strongly wish Jerry didn't feel this way, for with few people have I so quickly built up a series of sentimental connections. How wrong to proudly go telling everyone about our ballet, and how blushful when it doesn't come off! *Tant pis!* Mostly it's order I want; I loathe things left hanging. I lose such order in drinking (maybe even in writing music) that in my conscious life I have a phobia. No love note thrills me half so much as a musical fan letter from a stranger. But once the letter is read I sink back to where I was, because I've never been much interested in hearing my own music played: it embarrasses me, like standing naked before a crowd which suddenly sees that you have just one leg (if only they knew about my internal organs!). . . I'm not sure what "happiness" means to me; I *do* know that unfortunately it's never a situation of the moment, but rather a condition of sensual perfection which I'll achieve when I "grow up"—that is to say, *never*. . . I don't suppose he'll believe me, but I'd like Jerry to think in later years that I really loved him.

An army cannot be made from a group of people of which each one is different. And how we change every hour! I don't mean that yesterday my hair was peach colored, tomorrow sea green. It's a change interior, unrealizable because of Time; we all breathe the same molecules which metamorphose even as we do: we can't *see* them because we *are* them. For instance: two people sit and talk; the man leaves the room for twelve minutes; but, at the start of these twelve minutes, it's arranged that—for the woman in the room—Time stops: she is frozen, Time too. This arrangement ends at the man's return. Now the woman is twelve minutes behind him (as though she'd been born twelve minutes before the universe). She will literally not recognize the man. . . Julius Caesar could never inhale our air. How much more complex is the ebb and flow of our relationships from lack of understanding! Can we recognize the stars from night to night, which change their sense as we approach? How can I know if the blue I see today is the blue of yesterday, unless yesterday's comes back to stand beside today's? Can we have two simultaneous

Times? How can I know if my blue is yours? When may we be sure of what may turn false? Some words I pronounce in a curious way because my mother pronounced them thus when I was learning to speak. To me this is the right way, though it is called wrong by the world. And still the Arab and the Manhattanite are as knotted together as Siamese twins.

From the threads of so many methods the same desire for expression is woven. Who but researchers (those I hold most in contempt) care where a masterpiece comes from as long as it comes? Which doesn't keep me from writhing in envy at the methods of others—I want only what isn't mine. I, too, change, and remain the same. Why, yesterday, did I—the image of order—burn my hand six times, either in lighting the stove or in putting out my cigarettes? Today I haven't burned myself. *Passons. . .*

Gide said that at twenty-five he knew already all he had to say; the remainder of his life would be dedicated to saying it. He got up early, saw beauty in everything, worked regularly, sought love at specific hours, didn't drink, wasn't bored. So he is accused of living out his era in ignoring "major issues." Cannot we have great men with happy natures, to whom the writing on major issues does not seem writing, since everything changes? For me, I like things to stay as they are; it is I who would move among the frozen landmarks. Yet I work by crisis and devote myself to garbage like so many now.

❧

Ohana, not being *chez lui*, I left him a note and took a walk through the Mamounia gardens. It's almost indecent, this January weather. The paths are heavy with hot smells like living inside of an orange (Venice is like strolling through the veins of a dead woman). Personally I never just stroll (despite what I used to tell my parents after supper, with the excuse that I was a melancholy poet) though I do walk a lot, always in suspicious parks looking for encounters which haven't materialized since I was fifteen; my happiest love was then because I didn't know danger, and danger can't plunder innocence. Yet at that age I was much more the Corrupter than now. With that shyness, how could I have dispelled our high-school poetry club with just a lyric about lesbians? My passivity was always stronger than other people's aggression. . . At that age too we all had special modes of expression, like saying "this" for "that" (*"This* is very interesting" instead of *"That* is very interesting"). After all these years then, I was nonplused in Paris to come across an American intellectual of eighteen who exclaimed: "What! You live in Marrakech? But don't the nightingales drive you crazy?" I had forgotten how the hideous style of the young never changes from generation to generation.

On the way back from Tangier, I went into the monstrous church of Rabat. There were just four other people there, and I watched them. French Catholics cross themselves more slowly than Americans; they do it as I used to in imitating what to me was a mystery but what was just habit to others: the movement of the hand, from forehead to chest to left shoulder to right, traced a burning thread which stung itself into the flesh, then faded like a headache with aspirin, or the smoke of a forest fire. . . The first time I was in a Catholic church I must have been nine: Mother took me (on Chicago's 55th Street) with my sister to witness the mass for our "education." How different it was from the hard chairs, the frigid silence of our Quakers! What surprised me most in this fog of gold incense, was a strange woman in rich blue wool, with wonderfully manicured hands joined in prayer. That beautiful person was A CATHOLIC (magic word, lucky person!). Until then I had imagined all Catholics wore rags, that only Jesus had a right to sparkling robes.

I don't know why, but Sex has always been the favorite topic of every intelligently cultured person I've known. The favorite topic for every *un*intelligently cultured person I've known is Books, or, what is worse, Music. Casablanca is the sexiest of towns: the air swims with it. I had to hurry home and resume work to forget all this. Only to find, in the middle of the sunny Place Jemâa-el-Fnâa, an ostrich which will swallow any coin smaller than a five-franc piece. Tomorrow morning his masters will search his excrement for their reward.

Last night I had a dream. Two small dogs fighting became two fighting boys. One ripped out the eye of the other. A voice said: "Then two bluish strings hung from the hole's edge, like remnants of a rotten egg flowing out of the broken shell."

Today's Maggy's birthday.
Ten years ago my favorite foods were sweet potatoes (with marshmallows), beer (Milwaukee's best "amber fluid," as Dick used to say), and cherry pie (with the crumbling, tan crust that only Olga could make). But not at the same time.
I like to fill ash trays just in order to empty them. . . Am attracted by people who are attracted by Youth; in twenty-two years I'll be fifty; and then what.

I saw the spirit's fire once or twice, but only long ago during childhood's discoveries. With growth of technique and its cluttering of the mind I hear things differently; the wide-open door through which I once saw brilliantly has become a hairline. I work more and more toward the *clarity of youth* which proportionately recedes. Death is quick, life long. Our greatest discovery is in dying. How then will it benefit us? Learning is for living.

The same piece of music alters at each hearing. But oh, the need to repeat and repeat and repeat unchanged the sexual experience.

I loathe Marx's "Religion is the opiate of the people." Yet the statement is true and thank God! Marx meant this with shallow cruelty; but the Church, with all its bloody history, has given magic and poetry for two thousand years. I think if the Quakers had offered incense to my childhood I might not be a composer today.

Elliott Stein and I are writing a new libretto. Maybe we should call it *Father of the Sphinx Killer*. It's about Oedipus' father. In the legend, Laius was banished from his native land for kidnapping a boy. He fled to Greece, and thereby introduced pederasty to that country for the first time.

I'd like to do a third opera in the form of a comedy on Saint-Germain-des-Près with a Negro contralto singing the blues with an oboe. Also perhaps a "Grand-Guignol" melodrama, ridiculously bloody. These operas will all have the same instrumentation, and should be performed by school children. The one on Oedipus will have only two men's voices; the sound of men is less tiring than women: the former sing more in their speaking tessitura. The son will be the bass and the father the tenor. Why not? The bass will sing high, the tenor low—the tension will petrify. The first words—"Father, tell me. . ." As much suspense as in *Sorry, Wrong Number*. A keyboard orchestra (that Lou Harrison used to dream of): harmonium, organ, piano, celesta, glockenspiel, two harpsichords, three clavichords, plus four bass flutes in unison. . . I want an aria on sexuality (description of touch) sufficient to "erect" the audience, an aria on cruelty (description of blood) sufficient to scare the audience, and an aria on nostalgia (description of past springs) sufficient to make the audience cry.

❧

But I've heard nightingales sing and it's not so beautiful as all that.

❧

Received today from Paul Bechert a subjective letter bawling me out (good-humoredly) for how I "make people suffer"—except for *him*. Then he adds: "I don't really need you, because the world is full of fascinating, capricious creatures like you. But I think you need me. No one else tells you the truth about yourself. I do, and always will." Jesus! How many people have told me *that* in my life? Fifty maybe? Seventy-five?

❧

Guy recounts a disease (or rather a perversion) he has observed in certain Cheleuh tribes: the compulsive eating of soil. An otherwise normal citizen is attracted, not by food, but dirt. Desire for nourishment is as foreign to him as a lesbian's for a sailor. His family forces him to eat, as he has lost all instinct for self-preservation.

❧

During the two years before puberty (simultaneously with my craze to become a Catholic) I collected birds. Live birds, in an array of cages I made myself: cages of wicker, or metal bars, cages of glass, all huge and containing miniature forests of ferns and twigs. . . My passion for ornithology was ferocious; I knew all the Latin names (but wild birds didn't interest me, only domesticated). Now I just remember the standard names: Strawberry Finches, Cordon Blues, Red-billed Weavers, Gold-necked Weavers, Java Rice Sparrows, Gouldian Finches (these were the most sensational), Society Finches. When we were in Paris in 1936 I took many more home from the bird market on the Ile de la Cité; they cost nothing. I spent hours, months, spellbound before the great cages, watching the slightest movement of my multicolored parakeets, my dwarf parrots. (These were the hours, months, I later spent alone figuring what music was all about.) I was disdainful of canaries. . . They would breed. We would let them fly loose in the living room among the sunny plants. Sometimes a surprised visitor's poised teacup would be spattered by droppings as a feathered friend whizzed by. I had names for them taken from my reading: Ichabod Crane, Edmond and Mercedes, Zeus and Hera. Cosette and Marius were a pair of Zebra Finches (the female is the more beautiful: about half the size of a canary, all pearl-gray plumage with a bright orange beak). We gave them vast amounts of cotton and they built a nest as elaborate as a beehive, high up behind a bust of Shakespeare on the bookshelf. Cosette laid one egg which never hatched. She later died. Marius committed suicide; that is, we brought him another mate soon after and they killed each other. This was my first heartbreak. My life was birds: I belonged to bird clubs, went to bird shows, subscribed to bird magazines, wrote to the bird farms of California to send me live shipments of their rarest specimens (most of which originate in Australia). I sought avicultural references in all of life's variations the way a thrilled masochist looks for murder in the daily papers. I heard that Chinese emperors blinded nightingales to make them sing by day. I stole the sky-blue Robin's egg from the Vermont farm of our poet friends the Hendrichs, who were also pacifist, and did not believe in theft. The smell of summer was the light of birds to me, and I hated people who didn't know the word "Bird". . . Then, almost overnight, as my voice changed into adolescence, I lost interest. I put all these creatures into one cage, took them downtown to Vaughan's Seed Store (anyone named Vaughan was magic to me) on Chicago's Randolf Street, and sold the bunch for seventeen dollars. With this money I bought two record albums: *Skyscrapers* of Carpenter, and *Le Sacre du Printemps*.

I was thirteen.

❦

Passed an almost perfect day in Mogador with Hélène Rémy. Two touching dramas took place.

We went to the sultan's castle, deserted in the seventeenth century, a few kilometers out of town, crumbled on an immense beach. No one is near, just sand and the sea. The whole palace is invaded by sand: the roof is gone, and you walk from room to room and in and out of the windows on hills of sand. The stone walls seem torn like paper, and half the building has disappeared beneath the sand streaked with tiny footprints. Then Hélène came running toward us with something cupped in her hands: a baby rabbit, numb with fright, his ears flat against his head, his nose bruised, and his little hind paws crushed and dry with blood. We examined the sand on the floor of a roofless room and found traces of what seemed a battle with an eagle who must have taken the rabbit in his claws, then dropped him from high. . . What were *we* now to do with this dying thing? We considered a series of possibilities, then decided. A thousand yards away on the edge of the ocean was an old fort eroded from the center and slumping outward on every side like a cake that has failed. We crossed slowly to it on the long stretch of beach—a funeral procession in the stifling light, the quivering animal with just enough strength to make his eyes gleam. We climbed high onto the ramparts which literally hung lopsided into the waves. We paused a long sad time, reasoning, looking at the moss in the sun. And then, with all our force, we hurled the baby rabbit out to the air where he twirled for a moment in the brightness, then was flung by the wind into the ocean. He was certainly killed instantaneously by the blow. We were depressed. We came back past the sultan's forgotten castle, filled now with wind as evening was approaching.

In the city proper we went again to the white-walled cemetery (filled mostly with Spanish and English children dead two hundred years ago) built right on the sea. But we were asked brutally to leave by the guard who discovered us standing on tombstones and peering over the wall onto the wild beach, which was littered with large rocks of orange, heavy blue and brown, like Braque. . .

Tonight I am all alone. The lights down in the city are beginning to come on, and the dogs in the Médina are yelling. There's quite a wind. Mésäoud has fixed me a good supper (veal, watermelon, *thé à-la-menthe*) but he's now gone, though he offered to spend the night in case I were afraid. And I *am* a little afraid. Any *indigène* who felt like it could come and cut my throat—no doubt with reason. . .

We've been listening ten times a day to Ralph Kirkpatrick's "long-playing" version of Falla's masterpiece. Years ago I had the composer's own recording, and it seemed more savage and raw, a kind of Spanish Kafka in music. Ralph is slicker, but the harpsichord doesn't make enough noise. . . It's funny how one knows that certain masterpieces must have been totally conceived in a single day. These three movements overflow into each; it *had* to be written quickly so as not to spill on the floor and disappear. Think of the great works that have been forgotten in dreams—that have been known to just one person! My best works have burst from me like a lonely infection that finally splits the skin. Pieces I have slaved over have always been artificial failures. That's my way of working. Schubert's too. It has to do with poetry already written. I mistrust Poulenc when he says he sweats out every song: I'd like to know how *Figure humaine* was written (I'll ask him, next time we meet *en promenade* between the two confessionals of the Luxembourg). . . Beethoven was different. I'll never forget Xénia coming home wilted after her first hearing of the *Missa Solemnis*. "How could he write such a thing? He was just a man." Just a man, she said, with tears in her voice.

A letter from David Diamond who writes: "I want you always to remain a dedicated craftsman. . . I hope Janey Bowles is continuing to write as she's immensely gifted!" *Dedicated craftsman, immensely gifted,* these phrases turn my stomach, the same as (years ago at school) the expressions: *Play the game!* or *sense of responsibility.* To whom would I be responsible, were I to know the sense of the word? *Je ne puis guère croire qu'il y aurait davantage de crimes si nous n'avions plus de lois.* And a craftsman is the last thing *this* composer wants to be. David's splendid technique is exactly the reason he may not go down in the history he's planning. I prefer Satie who had no technique, therefore no responsibility. Certainly technique and gift together don't make genius. The combination is inhibiting.

Composition is notation of distortion of what composers think they've heard before. Masterpieces are marvelous misquotations.

Tonight as I packed Guy said, deeply moved:

"If anyone saw you packing your bags like that, he'd never suspect your self-satisfaction which is, *au fond*, quite superficial. It's feigned, and to protect yourself. You who have no home, who leave me in order to settle with others in any old hotel room! With only those disgusting pants, and that ugly briefcase which hides your latest *chef-d'oeuvre* on which you worked so hard! How many people, less important than you, enter a house like a whirlwind and leave it the same way, worrying about their clothes and their affairs of the moment! And I, who want to build a new house only so that you might live there, with your own piano! But it's clear that despite all your airs, you just live for music. You need so little luggage, you make so little noise in leaving, like birds who fly away. I'm going to weep."

Tomorrow I take the plane from Casa to Paris. I don't think it will crash. I must be back before the twentieth as my passport (I only have a temporary one since the theft last September) expires that day. And I must cash my Fulbright check and resume the classes with Honegger. I have exactly 2,080 francs. . . I am nervous, excited, embarrassed at the pleasant thought of seeing Marie Laure and three hundred other friends, and the dentist and his drill and his bill. Though what is my uppermost idea? Shall I admit it? It is the wonder of how my first *fine-à-l'eau* will taste after seven weeks of abstinence.

It is warm and cloudless.

Part 6
Paris: 1952

For more than a week I've been back in Paris, and the horrors here are even worse than those of Casablanca where the streets were lined with rioting Moslems screaming *Indépendence!* Perhaps in ten years Casa will be deserted, crumbled, no more than the old sultan's sandy palace on the Mogador beach.

On the airplane were twins: frightful girls covered with lipstick and long hair and heavy bellies. With them was a third girl, shorter and older, but dressed and painted identical to the other two. The three were obviously part of a circus. Their absolutely similar ugliness was stultifying. (I thought of Karl Shapiro's "Mongolian Idiot," and of D. H. Lawrence's "Elephant.") And yet what envy, what solace, what total mutuality in their caresses, their breasts, their *tutoiement* lisped quietly.

. . . nothing is worse than death. And if one consoles oneself that death is the end of all, it's also certain that nothing is worse than life. Why work, why bother? For of that which was Nikolai Nikolaievitch nothing remains. (Tolstoy on his brother's death)

My order and actions are conscious in spite of myself, and nearly all in defiance of death. With every street crossed I say, Well I wasn't hit *that* time; with every cigarette I say, Well I've managed to smoke one more before dying; with every letter written I say, Well at least it's in the mail and even if I die someone will exclaim: "To think I received a note from him the day after his death!" So I cross more and more streets, smoke more and more, write more and more letters—always trying to increase the number of living gestures between myself and my death. Whenever a work is finished death feels closer, which is why I must launch myself immediately into a new one. For the idea of dying in the middle of unfinished business seems not only indecent, but impossible. That I should die while others live is insupportable, but is nevertheless the force that blasts me forward into actions monotonous and useless, into other actions performed even while saying: If I don't do this thing, then I'll have died without having done it, and though it bores me and saps my strength, my strength is still stronger than myself.

I suppose this is why I keep a diary (or let myself be painted, fornicated, led into foreign countries). Fear of being forgotten is so compulsive I'd like to be remembered for each time I go to the bathroom, and I'd even prefer not to go alone.

Lunch with George Bemberg and Raffaello de Banfield, the richest boys in the world, who (after a penetrating conversation on the sorrows of our world) quibble about the division of the check to such a degree that I paid for all three of us.

Patricia Neway tells me she sang three of my songs on B.B.C. last month, but she can't remember the titles.

Work going well (*The Resurrection*). But of this one mustn't write in a journal, or the music itself will never be realized.

Have just learned that I must leave this apartment (75, rue de Vaugirard) as the building has been confiscated by priests!

Last night I read *Les Cenci*. It would make a wonderful movie-opera. Stendahl himself speaks of Francesco Cenci as a ghastly Don Juan character. There are pages of good form, terror and beauty and detail, especially at the end. Beatrix' words are heart-rending: *"Comment est-il possible, ah! Dieu! qu'ainsi à l'improviste je doive mourir?".* . . . Perfect for singing. . . The machine of execution called a *mannaja* (is it a Spanish word?) sounds uglier than the electric chair. A kind of guillotine, the footnote explains: *"La mannaja devait ressembler à l'instrument de mort français."* It's as though one said: Like an octopus, only worse!

Before going to see Julien I had the weird pleasure of meeting Iris Adrian in flesh and blood, at the St. James bar (drinking ginger ale, which I haven't seen for three years). Said she, "I don't care *who* you are, but I like you anyway. Sit down!" (It was Margaret Bonds' friend Muriel Landers who introduced us; they're singing together in Jack Benny's show which is touring Europe. I was with Elliott, who explained to me that I. A. had made three hundred movies, always taking the part of a dumb blonde, notably in "Blondie" pictures, and in *Lady of Burlesque* with Barbara Stanwyck.) "And I hope to make three hundred more," said Iris. "There's a lot of laughs in that racket. And a lot of tears!" Her hair is so blonde it's silver; she must be forty. She continues: "So you're writing an opera! Hope you make money. In show biz there's only two kinds of audiences: the kind you got, and the kind you don't. The kind you don't got don't pay off, and I don't care *how* good you think your opera is. . . You fellows live in Paris? You must speak a little French by now? Why'd you leave the States? Of course it's easier for a guy to live away than for a girl when you've got a husband and children.". . . She says "children," not "kids," showing she takes marriage very seriously. Her voice is loud, sad and steady. She drops her cigarette and speaks to it as it lies on the floor: "God-dam you! I'll get you back. Don't just lay there looking back like that! You won't get away from *me*. . . Write for television, boys. *That's* what pays off.". . . I go away feeling touched, knowing these girls live with their mothers. Why should I explain that our paths and standards vary?. . . I relate all this to Julien who doesn't think it's funny. He is too French for the American myth and magic of the movies. Elliott is in seventh heaven.

On the Boulevard des Batignolles last Sunday night was a bicyclist who (walking) turned three times to look at me, then vanished. For my part this was a love I will never forget. Unhad love is sweeter.

Lunch today at Robert de Saint-Jean's. Cocteau arrives in dungarees—the excuse being he's between rehearsals (*Oedipus Rex* at the Champs-Elysées). Fine food, and a finer monologue by the guest of honor. Julien finally manages to exclaim: "Really Jean, you should have a Boswell!" Jean retorts: "Yes, but it's not all mine. For instance, did you know? it wasn't I, but Péguy who said: *Il faut savoir jusqu'où on peut aller trop loin.*" (We must know how to go too far.) Why has he never admitted this in print? Then again, why *should* he?

To be in a police car taking you to prison, and by accident to drive past your own house where your mother is innocently sweeping, and expecting you home from school! To be in your father's car taking you to church, and by coincidence to drive past the place (a bar, a bench) where last night you fell in love!

Sauguet phones to ask if I'm free to write a ballet about *Dorian Gray* in collaboration with (of all people) Jean Marais.

It seems Marais will control, Cocteau-fashion, all but the musical elements: write the scenario, supervise the choreography, design sets and costumes, and mime the decaying picture. The hour-long production will be premiered less than two months from now in Barcelona. I love pressure. I accept.

On my floor here at 75, rue de Vaugirard (which I must soon leave forever), there are five nationalities: to the left a German student learning his father's trade of manufacturing slate for roofs (and who, through the thin walls, hears me at love more often than I hear him); at the end of the hall, next to the *lavabos*, a Turk who is *en proces* with the landlady and who has a room full of kindling; at the other end a French couple (I have never seen them); across, a Chinese who has a French mistress; on my right, Henri; then myself, American. . . My own room is large and rather *chichiteuse,* aglimmer with color and plants, a ladder and bedspread given me by Marie Laure, several por-traits of myself, books, my own music conspicuously on display, and framed drawings Cocteau did for me. The contrast of Henri's room excites me; I go in there each noon (when I get up) for coffee and *croissants* if I don't have a hangover. There is nothing but the dull hotel furnishings which have always been there, and the drably marvelous and distant odor of dirty socks; a broken tube of shaving cream and an unmade bed that speaks. Across the room a clothesline hung with white shirts and shorts. Henri is away in Malakoff working since six-thirty in the morning, but I drink his coffee sitting in his armchair, smoking my Chesterfield in my red bathrobe with great monk's sleeves, and think about how Americans are clean and the French dirty, and go wild.

2 A.M. Heavy, moonless night. Even the rue de Vaugirard seems dead. Feeling alone, panicked at amorous responsibilities,

awed at abilities to smash. Henri has long since gone to sleep next door.

Noon next day. Shortly after writing the above I went to bed and a few hours later awoke from the realest nightmare of my life. If I write it here (a thing I never did during psychoanalysis) it's because, still trembling, I must shake it from me. . . I was alone here in my dark room, and walking to the window I looked down into the street instead of which I saw a black lake where nuns and priests were drowning in their effort to reach the door below. I knew I must leave before dawn and was waiting only for Henri to come. He lifted me in his arms and at the speed of a herd stampeding carried me down an endless road of poplars whose leaves hit my face in passing. A bleak day was breaking as we arrived into a huge room which resembled an empty theater, or rather an arena. Three or four ushers were cleaning up, and refused to speak to us, or in any way help us to escape. Henri had grown tall and blond. I had forgotten how to fly which generally I am able to do. The only road out was on the side of a mountain, but this was blocked by the hind legs of a beautiful and strong orange horse. I was told he would not kick, but after we had passed he began to kick ferociously. Once more in Henri's arms we descended a deep circular staircase with banisters of living eyes. And then, in my dream, I awoke. Total blackness. I ached horribly, especially in the mouth and on the right side of the abdomen as though I'd been kicked. On touching my face I realized I was drenched in blood. I also realized I'd fallen to the floor, but was relieved in knowing the pain came from the fall and not from an attack. Some very real accordion was playing a loud German waltz. I wanted it to stop. In spite of the wounds I managed to turn on the electricity—and this was the awful moment: my room had been transformed, transformed as only a dream could do. The two armchairs were nailed (or glued) to the ceiling, the floor was littered with thousands of

blades and tacks which cut my feet, the walls were streaked with
the painting of insanity, and the whole had been redecorated in
shiny black and orange Chinese furnishings. I knew it was
myself who had done it all while sleeping, who had risen and
worked with a somnambulist's swiftness. The blood was thick
as velvet all over my body; staggering to the mirror I saw my
reflection white as paper with the eyes of a madman staring back.
I went down the hall to awaken Henri and show him my room,
but was too numb with fright to speak. So I wrote with my
finger in the dust on the Chinese screen these letters: S A N G.
And Henri said: *"Va te rinser la bouche, elle sent le sang."* He
then turned into a woman and began to sing the waltz I'd heard
earlier. His singing was so loud that I gestured for him to hush,
but he only smiled as if to say: I wasn't singing, you only thought
I was because you've gone crazy. He was standing by the door.
Blood began to flow into my eyes. When it cleared away Henri
had vanished as quickly as a bird. . . Then I woke up in a
paralyzed sweat, turned on the light, looked at my watch: it was
ten to five (the hour in my dream which was scheduled for my
flight). The right side of my abdomen and my mouth ached
horribly. Summoning the courage to get out of bed I went down
the hall to wake Henri, so that he could come and sleep his
remaining few hours with me. He did, comforting me with his
arms as I cried and cried and cried and cried.

A cool and languid lobster lunch at Marie Laure's with
Poulenc who is witty and bright and religious and knows it and
you know he knows it and say so and it's a bit spoiled.

Lunch again *chez* Marie Laure who is so ill she couldn't come
out. We are worried but it is natural; she herself thinks she's
dying which of course means she isn't. . . Later went to Julius'

to hear him do my sonata before he records it for Decca next week. I don't like the work much anymore and would not have the nerve to write it today, but Henri found it *"très bien, qu'elle coulait comme un chapelet entre les doigts"*. . . . A filthy dinner in Raffy's where some strangers recognized me and stood at our table to talk. As always, I was terribly flattered, but affected matter-of-factness, which, if I could see it from afar, I would find despicable. . .

Marie Laure says that my French is a cross between that of the Princesse de Clèves and Jean Genet; that my accent is Russian; that I write it nearly as fluently as English but with a quite different personality.

What does a boy soprano have that even a Tiena Lemnitz lacks? I think it is that hollow white French pure sound of Trust; all the more exciting as we would like to hear it defiled. The *Ave Verum* of Fauré. Nobody can say anything more beautiful than the Gregorian exists. But as I listen to it I cannot escape the blond notes of credulity answered by low sonorities with black beards around them. This is sufficient for me to expire. My entire libido is based on this image of the dark which envelops the light. And I never forget my Norwegian ancestry.

At Lise Deharme's the young editor, Jacques Damase, all but dies as I enter, for I am the ghost of René Crevel. He's not the first to have seen this.

It is above all her voice which makes Lise Deharme the great lady. The sound of a whore in a room where she doesn't belong. You hear a rusty flower. Her parlor contains an emerald-colored carpet and six thousand plants, an aviary, a stuffed owl, countless oriental trinkets. The heat is atrocious. In this room she talks and wins hearts.

Six o'clock coffee with Francis Rose. His voice is his loss. I also suspect him of being a liar (a tragic liar, not a jolly one). However, he tells long tales of his son in prison, and in the end you are more afraid for yourself than anyone else.

Auric is alone in Paris for the others have gone to Spain. And so we spent the evening together at the restaurant Albert, rue de Grenelle. The poor man has been suffering so from gout for two weeks that he must use a cane. With his hat on I almost didn't recognize him when we met *aux Deux Maggots,* and it took us half an hour to walk five blocks. We spoke of what all musicians speak of: how we are cheated; the comparison of working habits; miserliness; public urinals; the excruciatingly hopeless trend the world is taking; who of our friends is bedding with whom and why; danger and love and the reasons for his own fame. But nothing private about him, and about me nothing personal. He talks well, and when he talks of the past he glows as though speaking to his son. But he is sad—in pain even—and his life is one of hinting. We drank a barrel of *muscadet* and then we stopped. I like Auric too well to say more, though I know this is a kind of cheating.

When I was fifteen, once after one of those trembling and tender adolescent disputes with my family, when the child has not yet enough logic for his heart's defense, I ran away from home (oh, just three blocks distance to Chicago's Century Hotel on 55th Street) and for forty-eight hours was *a bohemian.* And then I received a marvelous and comprehensive letter from Father telling me his understanding and why, and that the heart newly opened to freedom (which will *never* be) is ignorant. So

I returned home, crumbled in tears, to my family's arms. I'll be always the prodigal son as long as I live away from America, and landmarks, any arms I find along the way, are just substitutes for Father's. Unfortunately arms are a comfort only when they are being a comfort (that is the *present*); one cannot go about daily chores handicapped by pairs of open arms.

Nadia Boulanger writes me: *"Vous êtes doué, merveilleuse-ment. Puis-je me permettre de redire 'qui veut faire de grandes choses doit longuement songer aux details.' La citation n'est hélas exacte que dans l'esprit. . . Tous mes profonds voeux pour que vous fassiez* tout *ce que nous sommes en droit d'attendre de vous. . ."* The underlined *tout* is her scary method of censuring my whole collection of private relationships.

But I *do* care what others think, and there are those who see me only as a sop (a "human rag" the French say). Or, if they know I write music, they wonder (without interest) why I should have collapsed at the Pergola in a pile of broken glass at eight in the morning. Heddy de Ré takes me into the Discothèque, brings over Daniel Gélin so he can tell me how moved he was by what I'd done to his poems (which are mediocre, though the music is agreeable). I pretend not to recognize him. . . To add to the horror, summer has really struck here, and the heat of a Paris dawn in August is intolerable when one is drunk. Not to mention its soonness: dawn hits the city towards four, illuminating the bloodshot eyes of friends, and their wrinkles filled with dirt.

Lise sits at the Flore; I go by; a stranger behind her says, *"Voilà Ned Rorem qui passe. Je l'ai vu l'autre soir, seul comme*

d'habitude, installé devant son demi. On aurait dit un ange déchu." According to Lise, this is the prettiest compliment one could receive.

Lenny Bernstein once said (it must have been at least eight years ago, "The trouble with you and me, Ned, is that we want everyone in the world to personally love us, and of course that's impossible: you just don't *meet* everyone in the world."

Back from Barcelona where *Dorian Gray* flopped ignominiously. Nevertheless, after the performance, backstage at 2 A.M., a hundred adolescent girls storm me with programs to autograph. Complacent among these adoring gigglers, I begin to sign. Then Marais emerges from his dressing room. All heads turn. In a flash they desert me like rats from a ship, and fall upon the star. I remain alone. One of them returns furtively—to snatch her pencil from my hand.

Paris is brimming with signs (printed, or simply chalked on walls) saying: GO HOME AMERICANS. One sees also—though less often—LES STALINIENS A MOSCOU. For we who are not French, it is unpleasant to come across them. Even the wealthy French never travel, feeling their own country and language to be superior to others; they therefore misunderstand the voluntary displacement of foreign colonists. The Communist element here is disheartening in its force, though I can only look at it with a certain irritation, since I have always found Communists individually charmless and without humor; they are using an inhuman procedure to humanize the world.

What do I think about Modern Music? Gertrude Stein answered about painting: "I like to look at it." I say: "I hate to listen to it." The reply is a reaction, not a judgment. Now I find myself ever less able to judge, ever more moved by reactions. The public? This summer I saw Picasso, after a bullfight in Arles, accosted with the gifts of live infants. With a stroke of charcoal he designs on a baby's naked ass, and returns this art to the parents. What will they do, skin the child? Refuse it a bath for decades? The musical audience, for better or worse, cannot possess and so cannot brag; it is reduced to judgment and no longer reacts.

The biggest insult an American can receive is: "He isn't *natural*; he's always playing a role." But from the moment we learn to talk we start an existence of unnaturalness; a few years later we decide more or less what our particular role is and play it the rest of our life. . .

At Julien's, we discuss "dirty words" and how we both prefer the slang to the "proper" term for sexual organs and primary acts. There are certain medical terms I would rather die than utter, whereas the familiar substitute appears naturally in my vocabulary of a child. The dirtiest words I know are J—— D——. With shame I admit that while drunk recently I allowed this person to drive me alone all over Paris; he must have spent 200,000 francs on champagne, tips, private entertainment and such ostentation, not a sou of which he would have disposed of on me as a composer. He told me his personal detectives had informed him I was a "pale-pink Communist," which is the most idiotic accusation I have ever received.

Jacques Bourgeois, who was a paratrooper during the war, recounts for us the details of throwing oneself from an airplane. The fear is basic, since even the insane have no desire to fall from high places. My twin cousins in the Coast Guard used to tell of suicides off the San Francisco bridge: how women, as they fell would moan slow and loud, "Why did I do it. . .?"

It has been seven years; seven years ago I began this diary in 1945, the September after the war. "Seven" is a good number, holy, the length of the Egyptian plague, and the itch; also the number of years Hans Castorp spent up in that magic mountain; there are also the seven deadly sins and the wonders of the world; it is the age of which the priest says, "Too late. If you had given me your son at six I could have made him a Catholic; now he is formed, and should he have a vision it would not be one of ours.". . . Seven could doubtless be high time for me to cease such writing, but Marie Laure just gave me this little book, which she got in Holland, and said, "Write! For if you feel hideous afterwards, it is nonetheless pleasant while the hand is in motion."

Is this diary dishonest? Should I write here now? or go out and *do* something that should be written about? Still, one shouldn't write about what one does, but what one thinks about what one's done. Or should have done. So I'll write here now.

Ethel Reiner maintains that, for us, there are only five thousand people in the world, and sooner or later we meet them all. That's brutal.

Julius Katchen has read these diaries. "There are two conspicuous absences," says he. "Your love affairs and your family." What could I say of my family that would not be sacrilegious betrayal? This is for novels. It is not the place of a journal to investigate cores, but to discuss the misery of effects. I have no courage to go deeper: I would scare myself (as I used to, as a child, making weird faces in the mirror) and I want to be happy: without that I can't work. . . Love affairs, that's different. If I spend more time alone with those with whom I am in love than with even my dearest friends, it is nevertheless a different kind of time, like that of creation about which I never write. This is a period removed from Time and, like the act of love, has no limits, no beginning nor end.

The days are shorter, darker, already much colder: going-back-to-school weather. Bookstores display a sign *Rentrée des Classes* and windows full of rulers, erasers. The square of St. Sulpice steams with leaves and the Concorde is surrounded with rusty orange as I prepare with terror to leave this country. Had tea alone in Smith's today reading Bernanos. Next week I depart for America.

Part 7
Paris: 1953

Three months in New York were expensive. To save money, I've accepted Jacques Damase's invitation to stay *chez lui,* and ten years ago this bohemianism would have suited my fancy fine; but today my hands are too blue-cold to touch the keys; we hover around the stove, the floors are strewn with old magazines on top of which are plates caked with last week's eggs; the *"bidet"* is thick with slime; there are dead flowers and crumbling manne-quins and dust and broken windows and lighted candles every-where, and cold, cold, cold. I groan to feel my head so full of ideas and unable to notate them because of the squalor. If I don't notate them now, when will I? Life is passing. To escape the atmosphere I go out and drink (Monday, for the first time in twenty-three days!) only to return at 6 A.M. exhausted and too tired to care about the water's being turned off. The housing problem in Paris is beyond belief, and if I don't soon get a prize or commission or money of some kind, I'll be forced to suicide. In this frozen mess, Jacques plans to give me a cocktail party on Saturday, though I have no desire for that lost array of congealed faces I'd hoped to avoid by plunging into work far from New York. Marie Laure I see often (tomorrow we go to Desgobert's, the lithographer, to make some song covers), but she is concerned with a life far from mine without temperance to tolerate my lack of interest in the outer world. But this city is far from the South of France where eventually we'll find each other again. My one pleasure is Henri, but love is not so much the memory of shared pain as of happy days. Poverty destroys all, the heart included.

Just in order to live Henri must rise daily at six, spend ten hours in Malakoff, then pass four hours of conscious liberty before retiring. This is mysterious to me: it does not permit alcohol.

Feeling low, and slightly high from fear of a war. Played my new *vocalises, chez* Marie Blanche on Sunday (long religious songs), and the French consensus is that I am a Protestant: no Roman would have set those words in that way (the *Holy Songs, Resurrection,* etc.). Poulenc's comment: "I find she sings better [Ethel Semser] since she has taken out her contact lenses and put on her regular glasses!". . .

Rather drunk then, and feeling low, because I make no money and feel no appreciation and have reached a point of stagnancy with no ideas. Would like to be really drunken, but haven't even the force to combat the rain. Everywhere is talk of a war.

Heddy has become the barmaid at Agnès Capri's (not to mention having fallen in love with Jay Harrison, making a social cobweb of the earth once more). Heddy *mixes* drinks these days, and (with Jay) asks too many questions about why love is love: that domain's more evasive than the sky. For me, I eat radishes and drink myself into a trance (radishes are a favorite trance food).

Today I learn from Mother's letter that once more I have *not* been granted the Rome Prize nor an Arts and Letters Fellowship. Next month we'll know about the Guggenheim, though I am sure to fail a sixth time. Why keep trying? It's not the idiotic recognition I want but the money: in nine months I'll be thirty, and though I feel I have a great deal to say, it seems that no one wants to listen.

Paris for a week has become radiant in an early spring; we can walk out in shirtsleeves, buds seem to spurt shiny before our eyes, and we too in the vernal jerking feel we're being born again—a terrible urge to say the same old words of love, but to new people.

Arthur Laurents asks: "I wonder what would have happened to Romeo and Juliet if they had lived.". . . But it is *because* they died that we know their names. Great love *must* die young. Beauty is beautiful because it cannot endure. If love lives on, it leads to middle-class quarreling. The potion of Tristan and Isolde was brewed to last only three years. Even the slabs of gold wore away from the pyramids.

It's been three weeks since I moved here to Marie Laure's— 11, Place des États-Unis—by far my best residence in Paris. It's all that keeps me alive, the thrill of being alone in a comfortable bed. Of course I'm in love, but, as we know, that has nothing to do with happiness.

Philippe Erlanger says that love is bestowing. But *I* am sure anyone can give; force is in receiving: *n'est pas aimé qui veut.*

In France, if I am invited to lunch on Sunday at the home of a middle-class family, there is always a deaf and friendly grandmother, hard heavy streaks of sunlight landing on abominable furniture, and the eldest son (with a little mustache) who, for the first time, feels pangs of love (whether he knows it or not) because I am there. Someone will whisper to him that I'm often given to excesses, which is why I'm not drinking today, and for months afterward he will not be able to concentrate on his lessons at law school.

❦

André Dubois troubles me when he says my work is too perfect, too serene, too refined, like Reynaldo Hahn; that in my music as in my (Quaker) life I have not said what I really desire—which is too bad since prettiness disappears at death. And André adds that Boulez has lost patience with the waste of such a talent. Honegger had faith in me, but he is not of my time. I am more intelligent than outsiders know, but less than friends think. *Pour moi, je ne suis pas assez fort pour savoir où doit aller ma génération. . .*

❦

I will not have the courage to say in this diary the things that should be said until I reach an age when the saying of such things will no longer be becoming.

❦

Stella Adler, who pretends never to recognize me, explains that all "goyem" look alike to her.

❦

Sam Barber is in town again, rather sad and unenthusiastic, though witty and sympathetic. He tells of Copland's interview with McCarthy. Copland, after a dignified explanation as to why he had lent his name to certain lists, suddenly realized that McCarthy didn't know who or what he was.

❦

Bernac, too, seems sad and older, but showed interest in my new French cycle which he plans to sing in Fontainebleau. . .

Since coming to Europe I have not written more than three songs equal in expression to those of the New York years which I play now with a sense of "time-passed" and the notion that *another person* put those notes on paper.

With that poignance of retrospect, I have been going through the twenty-five or thirty letters received through the years from David Diamond and Paul Bowles. David's (obviously written for posterity) are those of someone *not* a writer: profound, self-conscious, poetic, full of advice, human and long. But Paul's (like Julien Green's) are of the dullest. Men of letters don't waste time writing letters.

The Paris weather, pale as death, continues as in January though July is nearly here. Everyone talks of the Rosenbergs.

Hot and cloudy. Yes, the Rosenbergs were electrocuted. Europe seems less sad than stunned. The Place de la Concorde is filled with police cars half-heartedly preventing crowds from throwing rotten eggs at the American Embassy. Every free wall bears a poster caricaturing Eisenhower's famous grin: each tooth is an electric chair. Martyrdom is unbecoming to those who impose it.

Henri Hell, who has already read the just-published Rosenberg letters, says they aren't those of guilty people. Yet who believes himself guilty who has acted through conviction? Naturally the letters are sincere, pathetic. Besides, guilt isn't guilt until discovered. How many think me always drunk because they only see me thus, ignoring my thousand silent sober days? A drunkard is only a drunkard when he's drunk. Is a murderer a murderer only when he's murdering?

A cruel joke is circulating: Mr. Rosenberg, examining the electric chair, expresses interest and asks questions about its mechanism. The guard answers: *"Ne vous en faites pas, mon ami—on va vous mettre au courant."*

Marriage resembles the involuntary union of snakes—and something always comes between. A boa can swallow a pig, though it takes hours. A second boa can start swallowing the same pig from the other end. But their mouths eventually join and the larger snake swallows the smaller, like it or not. There's no choice: being locked together by a doubly half-digested pig, the little boa must smother, all writhing inside his rival's body.

All endings are sad, even the end of pregnancy. I resent my friends' wives who rob me of my friends, who end the meaning of this friendship. And all change too is sad, even a change for the better. Stars' meanings alter as we come near, but *we* never change really—though nothing stays truth in a third person's mouth.

What's new for the old is old for the new, so how do we know where we are? I mean, the old are new yesterday, the young today. A child, not having been born, can't see this. Yet an old person feels newer today than yesterday when he was younger. So things get newer as they grow older, because today is younger than yesterday.

Old's the opposite of new, but also of young. Old people are more recently old than the unborn, more newly old, newer, constantly on the crest of the wave, advancing, nearer to that future from which the young are distant. Antiques grow ever newer—new hags, a new crone. Newborn babies are all wrinkled with age.

Last month is older than today. Is today younger, or only newer? The past, now old, was when the world was young. So we become younger and younger as we continue on and away from that old time when the world in flames was brand new, and so very agèd it now seems. And we are newer, being more recent. . . Memories of the future, the ancient future.

Oceans are old and they don't wrinkle. Now Marie Laure corrects me: "Darling, oceans are nothing *but* wrinkles!" Well, I could wish forever to be nailed to those waves.

He is looking older and unchanged. (I am afraid of looking older if not changed.). . . But neither would I look changed and nobody has ever been changed and nothing ever changes, which is why fairy tales are about the turning of ducklings into beauties and pumpkins into coaches, and why children now take drugs—to ignore what seems to be an alteration in the world outside them.

I want so to notate these joys of the past, but hesitate, for fear the very words may themselves become memories to break the heart in later years. . . I feel happy. Unhappy only that all must change. Glad that nothing changes. I live so as not to be anonymous; how many say this? are they more content? Why must I evolve? Books don't—why must I? But books *do*, depending on the reader's age and the time he lives in. They change too in rereading, generally for the worse; when they change for the better it's not, unfortunately, because the reader is smarter, but because the book is older.

Styles, like skin, change every seven years but with such overlapping that we notice nothing. If only we could shed like snakes! or, like caterpillars, emerge from cocoons as butterflies into a new season of joy. Nothing again will ever be new, though every homecoming necessarily indicates a change. But the same voyage will always be new. Nothing is waste that makes a memory.

The hand that wrote me the burning letter is dead. Old letters die but we still remember. Finally we don't remember anymore. All passes. Beauty too. Masterpieces last longer (longer than living) though seen newly by new eyes, but they also disappear. Even continents, which are here the longest, must finally be washed away. The most exciting crotch won't stay that way, nor this paper, nor this ink. Will it all be back like our flying saucers in a universal circle?

Books have ends. But there's no denying the fact that the older I get the more past I'll have. The speed of that past, like the speed of the things of the earth, increases with the world's age, accumulates with the hysteria of a falling boulder.

It's painful, occasionally dangerous, to share a tender experience, for the future so quickly becomes the past where we find ourselves alone again. But without this sharing, how live? By molding silently that which the public will eventually snatch away to share among themselves? These sentimental sharings nonetheless take place every day despite us, and are accumulated in a nebulous attic from which we withdraw them in our old age and laugh.

Irène Joachim invited me to meet Kabelevsky (and Aragon with Elsa Triolet) at the *Maison de la Pensée Française,* and I went, taking Jay Harrison. Life being short, I prefer to ignore the consequences of fear; but it is much worse being bored to death, as we were. The intellectual Communist never changes, regardless of geography or generation. I reproach him most his lack of humor (not to mention his addiction to folksongs).

And I got drunk again with Heddy and Julius, starting toward midnight at the Steinway factory, in a room with twenty pianos, where we drank two cases of beer and played Satie until dawn.

We've now all read Huxley's new book on devils. There are those who get famous without caring for the publicity; others who care, but do not get famous. There are those who could escape death at the stake (Grandier) but do nothing to save themselves; others who would give any number of denunciations to escape the fire, but are burnt anyway.

To become famous I would sign any paper.

Monday night (rue Monsieur le Prince) I dined on melon, salmon, and apricot melba beneath a bouquet of orange gladiolas. This is a "hangover-type" observation.

Virgil at a *vernissage*: "There're so many pictures you can't see the people."

I am privileged to say *"The Moonlight Sonata,"* having passed from when one says it and shouldn't, to when one knows it's inexact, to the third convolution when one says it in jest without smiling because that's quicker than opus numbers. Similarly Ezra Pound says "ain't."

When I left America I was still a little boy; now I am not any more—except on certain days. It is hateful to recall long ago during an early week in Paris, sitting with John Cage and others at a summery café near the Sunday-night fountain of the Place St. Michel. We were laughing sweetly and literarily, when a rosy-cheeked middle-aged American gentleman sitting alone nearby came up to our table. "I just wanted to tell you young folks that it does my ears good to hear the English language,"

he said smiling, and went off. "How disgusting!" I murmured, with the assured superiority a new tourist feels when surrounded by friends in a strange land, himself already French, though ignoring the tongue (an attitude I notice in many countrymen who arrive in conquering hordes each June) and disdaining even lonely old men for being a week younger. "Why?" answered John, who had already read Henry James. And he was right.

There are two breeds of U.S. representative in Paris: those who look too American (crew cuts and cameras) to be anything but American, and those who look too French (berets and *Gauloises*) to be anything but American. Expatriates from "back home," no matter what their style (from besotted sexagenarians in Right Bank hotels, to youths at the Flore who've "forgotten" English, yet say only *merde*), are identifiable by their eyes—their credulous gaze, both embarrassing and wonderful. No Europeans have it, not even infants.

If, as I figure it, there are 531,460 hours in the life of a man who dies at seventy, will I (at the average of one whole day a week for the past twelve years) already, at twenty-nine, have been drunk during at least 18,000 hours of my life?

As a "serious" composer is this any more degrading than B.'s spending his years in dressing as a fine lady and prancing about to Nellie Lutcher records for our delight, or reading the letter-scene from *Traviata* to Stravinsky's Psalm Symphony? He and I just have different faces, different talents.

Once Stella Brooks took me to Julius Monk's on First Avenue, and I threw a beer bottle at a white piano because at that moment I didn't like white pianos on a summer night. The management locked me in the basement as dangerously insane (really) until the police came, and Stella pretended not to know me. . .

Late into last night I read Boulez' brainy article on the rhythm of Stravinsky. What opposites we are: he, pondering for months on the analysis of another's work (as I did at twelve); I, passing days pasting pictures into scrapbooks to glorify my own person. He makes me feel cheap, yet I neither admire nor approve of him.

As for my own work, I'm in a state of sterility. Not only have I no ideas, but no desire for work; nor any interest in the fact that I have no interest, desire, or ideas.

Spent the afternoon with Jay (who returns to New York tomorrow) at Poulenc's in that sunny high apartment on the Luxembourg, with chairs of orange plush and squeaking floors. Poulenc plays the role of Great Master more than any French composer, and he passed a witty hour giving details on his new opera to the Bernanos film scenario, which he'll take two years to complete before its La Scala production in Italian with Tebaldi, Duval, and others. I won't believe that he works with the amount of declared precision he pretends. His favorite interpreter in the whole world is Bob Shaw, whom he says has divined the speed of the very blood in his (Poulenc's) arteries. All the more surprising that Shaw is Protestant: *tendu,* and the *Stabat Mater* is Catholic: *calme.* . .

But I listen too closely to everybody and become confused (jealous) before such confidence. How difficult to follow one's own heart.

We write in diaries mostly when feeling bittersweet, and leave
a blank during periods of untroubled work. It's not always so
bad when one can dine out-of-doors on summer nights near the
French Theater, watching the fountain lights of the Palais-Royal
go on.

Talking with Henri of the tribe of Mau Mau and their current
behavior in Southern Africa, I say: "What *are* their tortures?"
He invents: "They snip a varicose vein at its base and pull it
slowly loose like a string the whole long length of the leg as the
victim shrieks." Imagine a person crucified face to the wood and
sodomized.

Here again my dishonesty is useless since the above devices
are without meaning unless I mention names: I am very well
aware who had veins, who was crucified.

"*Aimer les femmes intelligentes est un plaisir de pédéraste.*"
                              —BAUDELAIRE, Journaux Intimes

Marie Laure has come back too (so the ground floor was
reopened and I could take my first bath in three weeks—except
for the *bidet*), to arrange with the police about the fate of the
Balinese midgets who robbed the house with much publicity
a week ago and who, she thinks, live in the putrid belly of the
whale now on exhibition *aux Invalides*. Marie Laure is first of
all a child, second an artist, third a *vicomtesse*. (Isn't every artist
a cross between a child and a *vicomtesse*?) Fourth she is a saint,
fifth a masochist (because of Oscar), and sixth a bitch. (Isn't
every child an artist? and every child a mixture of saint and
bitch? and all *vicomtesses* bitches? and all artists saints?) In

short she has all it takes to make blood flow fast and far from
boredom. What I most hate is the nonimmortal quality of boredom. What I most like is intuition. . . She, like Cocteau, knows
about the beauty of beginnings and dangers of inertia; that art
today approaches science (not really, but really). Above all she
is generous, not to mention crazy. Aren't all artists and *vicomtesses* crazy? Though neither artists or children (and rarely
vicomtesses) are generous. In the three lunches I've had with
Cocteau (at Charles de Noailles's, Julien Green's, Marie
Laure's) I have learned little, but am educated rather by his
books. And this is true again of Marie Laure.

Man Ray has finished my three portraits. At his suggestion I
passed by his studio in St. Sulpice Saturday afternoon to personally scratch on the negative and add the inevitable soul's
calculation (a music staff, of course). I am unsmiling in the
dirty white raincoat and red scarf of Jerry Robbins. I like this
better than those of Georgette Chadourne, or Cartier-Bresson,
who made me look like an oriental orphan. . . Friday I'll be
thirty but the picture stays twenty-nine.

A moment ago midnight struck: it's the twenty-third of
October and at 2 A.M. I will be thirty. Just as a snake every
fourth season sheds his skin, so I learned when a child that man,
bit by unnoticeable bit, totally renews this largest of organs each
seven years. In those young days I longed for my fourteenth
(twice seventh) birthday, feeling that I then would walk about,
clean as on my first earth-day.

Then on the evening of the 23rd I of course got drunk: dining
with Henri *chez* Francis, Place de l'Alma, we begin with two

martinis each (the *apéritif*), a bottle of champagne with the meal, two or three Cointreaux in the Bar des Théâtres; then both on Henri's bike we roll to the Flore; two more Cointreaux at the Flore, two *aux Deux Maggots,* three or four beers with Terry McEwen on the rue Jacob; then Terry and I take a cab to the *Boeuf sur le Toit* to drink there God knows how much brandy and champagne, then the Club de Paris, then back to the dangerous Pergola till dawn and twenty beers and unremembered company and words. I wake next day feeling very much thirty with all my money spent and everyone else's. I take a ten-mile walk to collect my thoughts; toward midnight on the avenue Friedland a strong-faced sergeant says, *"Vous ne pouvez guère avoir bien plus que dix-neuf ans. Je n'aime, moi, que des mineurs!"* All this is a weekly occurrence, a weak and regular excuse for my cast-iron innards to distract me from my music, my correspondence. Yet is it not an improvement from the American and early French days when I'd begin at noon and keep on for four days?

Are there today no Americans in Paris getting famous as in the twenties? In residence are only Tom and Theodora Keogh, Jimmy Baldwin, Julius Katchen. Maybe me and Noël Lee. All the others were "known" before they got here.

Spent a recent Sunday at the *Moulin* of Hervé and Claude Alphand. The "country weekend" is foreign to me, and here was the atmosphere of the relaxed high French bourgeois telling long jokes of infidelity after lunch. Am I saved when Claude picks up her guitar and sings to us before the open fire? Claude, the wan, her pale hair; Claude made of expensive wax, all elegant in her lavender skirt, her purple knickers, her violet *espadrilles,* flat on her back again before the huge fireplace munching rosy bonbons from a box of gray crystal, her olive hair almost burning. Her intelligent voice moves us, but one can't sing all afternoon. And as nobody pays attention to me I'm bored, but can't leave, being far from home.

When will it snow?

André Dubois tells us that Poulenc has no awareness of the meaning of poetry (or literature) as an art. This is no doubt why he (Poulenc) writes such marvelous songs: he is concerned with words *only* inasmuch as they are connected with music. Auric, a real intellectual on the other hand, does not write successful songs.

Now I must go down to lunch. . . Who are the other guests? Marie Laure's husband Charles (a story in itself!), Pierre Barillet, Van Moppes, Francis Poulenc, Hélène de Wendel (*pour faire gai!*), Jacques Bourgeois. . . That will do. . . (Two hours later.) Lunch is over and I am no smarter.

Saw *La Corde* last night with Marie Laure dressed all in fancy black with her little black basket, like a shepherdess in mourning. . . We decided that though H. H. is physically dirty he is not mentally so; just disordered, as if instead of blowing his nose he swept his snot into a forgotten corner.

Who was next? Willy Kappell, and it was awfullest of all. Every American pianist in Paris was heavy with depression and I think none was relieved (relieved of his jealousy). Mother wrote me: "Nowadays when I hear of someone leaving this earth, it comes more as a surprise than a shock." But a plane accident:

is it *leaving* the earth? or, rather, returning with a crash? Perhaps the soul rises as the body descends, even while we live.

Some people experience their strongest joy in physical contact at the moment they have become jealous of their lover. Jealousy, I suppose, is what accounts for the excitement in a *partouze*. And the *voyeur* is jealous but overcomes it. In Sartre's *Baudelaire* there are countless examples for those of us who rationalize:

> *Of the intellectuals of his persuasion, he recognizes that "the more they cultivate the arts, the less they can get it up" which could pass for a confession. . . [And:] The voyeur does not expose himself; an obscene and discreet shiver runs over him, while, dressed to the gills, he contemplates nudity without touching it. He does wrong, and he knows it; he possesses the other from a distance, and he abstains.*

At lunch yesterday we talked about flying saucers (or at least *they* did—I never speak much) and science and robots that write poems and make love and calculate infinitely and are indestructable. And Thirion proved that the world (being an incomplete circle) will inevitably end in so many billions of years, etc., but hopefully by that time we'll have escaped to another planet. . . All this depressed me yesterday, but now I'm out of the mood.

At 3:30 Hugues Cuénod came to rehearse my *Poèmes pour la Paix* for the Swiss radio. He brought two pianists and a creole baritone named Salvador Thomas whom I clearly remembered as the narrator in Juilliard's production of Stravinsky's *Oedipus* in 1948, since it was on that very night that I broke out in chicken pox.

Spent the late afternoon going through my scrapbooks at Philippe Erlanger's hotel on the Quai d'Orsay. He says I'm a hundred years out of my epoch, my style being like Musset's *La nuit de Décembre*.

Then I went to pass a torturous half-hour at the wine party of a Korean poet in a miniscule hotel room, rue Jacob, where long-haired dirty American girls sat on the floor (though there were plenty of chairs), and Daniel Mauroc declaimed like a monotonous genius, and the invitation had been typed without capital letters. This *naïf* bohemianism took me back fifteen years to Chicago's 57th Street and Gertrude Abercrombie (dear to us all) and made me feel old.

Quiet supper with Henri who gave me a little radio to keep me company when I'm home alone nights orchestrating.

An awful cold. Slept badly.

Friday the thirteenth, and like yesterday the sky is purple, clear, cold, sunny. After lunch with Oscar my flu was at its worse, so I took a *corydrane* which made me float as I rehearsed my astounding "Jack l'éventreur" (poem of Marie Laure) with the lush Lescot for the party next month. A little American Negro mezzo (pupil of Bernac: they're *all* pupils of Bernac) came to hear us: she'd known me "by reputation" in N.Y. where she'd studied with old friend Mina Hager, but had imagined I was fifty. Everyone thinks composers are either bearded or dead.

Marie Laure has some marvelous new hose: transparent red, transparent blue. The red ones show legs that walked through a slaughterhouse, the blue show legs which have passed through clouds.

One of the stringy-haired girls that I mentioned above at the Korean's party, had said, "One's public is one's friends." This is certainly not true. Joan of Arc, burning at the stake, had plenty of public who were not her friends.

❦

The ASCAP journal is sent to me every once in a while—this time with an obituary column full of old pals: Albert Spalding, Berezowsky, Frank LaFarge (a sugary quack doctor for whom I feel no remorse), and Eric Delamarter, the gentle Chicagoan who had good words for me when I was an enthusiastic composer of fifteen. Now that I'm twice that age I've only banal ideas: it all comes out sounding like Tailleferre. I'm too young to go dry, except alcoholically speaking. The genius of Mozart eludes me, and he was more than a man. No matter how much instruction we receive, we will never comprehend more than what is already in us. When I am given praise for my work I feel I don't deserve it; I know too well my dishonesties, though what I've made that stays beautiful seems only natural. When I do not receive praise I feel the world is made of imbeciles. I require the sensations of Saint Anthony.

❦

No one—whatever his wish—can see himself growing older.

❦

The only poems I've ever really understood are those I've set to music.

❦

Quand j'étais jeune, on me disait: Vous verrez quand vous aurez cinquante ans. J'ai cinquante ans; je n'ai rien vu.
—ERIK SATIE

L'artiste contient l'intéllectual. La réciproque est rarement vraie.   —LÉON-PAUL FARGUE

❦

Coming back to my music after the usual dissipation is like returning to a starving dog—to a forgotten child for whom I'm responsible but haven't fed. It sulks and won't speak. And when we finally come to an agreement, it is with meaningless whines.

In New York where I used to drink for days on end, I would sometimes come home to find the child prostrate as a dead canary at the bottom of its cage without grain.

Then there are moments when this very remorse sets off a flood of inspiration, rich and thick as a hothouse tangerine, while periods of sobriety can be as dry as Ezekiel's territory, plangent with fake force and constipation.

Wish I could really learn to believe that the most expedient remedy for hangovers is abstinence.

My music *must* be instantly attractive; though I orchestrate skillfully, it is without chance or invention.

Finally saw Genet's movie. It was so much like everyone says that there's little surprise. (Jacob Wasserman's prison chapters were more remarkable but less pederast.) Creation is not based on experiences we've had, but on things we've imagined, woven, and finished: experiences we have not had. A great writer has not the time to live himself. . . Of course the best scenes (which F. Reichenbach projected on his wall, wrongly using Bartók for background) were not the out-and-out masturbation-without-climax "shots," but the smoke puffed into a straw, breathed and reabsorbed through the hole in a prison wall, from mouth to mouth by lovers who cannot, haven't, and will never see each other.

While watching the collection *chez* Balenciaga (whose mannequins are notoriously ugly), Marie Laure, at the appearance of one particularly frail gown, observes: *"Je peux bien me voir soûle dans cette robe-la!"* That also is my provision towards all attitudes I must assume.

❧

And as for Virgil Thomson, who has known me since eighteen, I can't forgive his two remarks made on the lack of immortality now starting to shine in my arteries:

1. Having encouraged me to invite Boulez out for a night of brandy so as to "find out" more about him (which I did), he later reports by telephone: "Do you know what Boulez says of you? He says only, *'Quel sinistre individu!'*"

2. Having spotted me last fall at a New Friends' intermission of the Stravinsky cantata with J. Le Sueur, he later phones to say: "I notice you're finally going out with *younger* people!"

Virgil, who used to remark (when I was shocked by what I thought was Lucius Beebe's anti-Semitism), "Sincerity is your big number, baby!"

❧

The phone: "But how will I recognize you?" "I'm beautiful."

❧

Why not: the composer as disappointed critic.

❧

Our fan for years, sweet Robin Joachim, name-dropper and lunatic, asks if he can dine with me. "Yes, but I won't be with a celebrity, just with a working-acquaintance." "Oh, that's all right," he answers, "some of my best friends aren't famous."

❧

I'll make this a *diary*, a daily report for awhile (a discipline, since in any case I'm writing no music these days).

Philippe Erlanger says that superficially I strike him as everything a good mother would *not* want her son to grow up to be!

Dined quietly last night at home with Marie Laure, and afterwards we went to Gaveau to hear Cuénod and De Menasce. Later (Marie Laure having returned alone to meet Oscar) I went to discuss the concert with Poulenc, Sauguet, Jacques du Pont and Henri Hell at the Critérion near the Gare St. Lazare, where Huysman's characters used to evoke London. I had a bad cold and Sauguet said I looked thin and hollow. My voice doesn't go with my face, the former being deep, the latter being fine. . . Wandered around St. Germain des Près talking long with fifty friends. Came home sober at 3:30 A.M.

Today slept till noon. Finished *The Duchess of Malfy*. Lunch with Cuénod (and his pleasant Swiss accompanist) to discuss his broadcast in Lausanne of my *Poèmes pour la Paix*. I'd already rehearsed them well last week with Perry O'Neil and Bernard Lefort; the latter will do them on tour with Germaine Tailleferre. . . After lunch went to *Thérèse Raquin* (Carné film starring Signoret looking weird) with Henri, and we were depressed by the heavy Lyonnaise atmosphere of bourgeois murder. We were supposed to be, too. . . Dined at the house with Marie Laure and Oscar. At nine had a date with an Arab near Cluny and made love three times in a filthy hotel room: not very sentimental, but it sweated away my cold.

On second thought maybe I won't make a daily report.

Marie Laure says moodily at least once a day: "Youth is what will still be here when we have died."

A nice autumn. Even prettier as seen from Poulenc's apartment overlooking the Luxembourg at the fall of a clear day. I

spent the late afternoon there yesterday with Henri Hell in order
to hear the *maître* sing us the first three and a half tableaux of
his opera. Beforehand we had hot lemonade and homemade
ginger cookies, and talked of the recent arrests in England of
Lord Montagu and John Gielgud. Then Francis played us what's
written of the *Carmélites* and I was disappointed. Usually I love
his music and feel he's the only one here who has not tumbled
into that touchy masterpiece-complex trap. Yet this whole
Carmelite idea seems so Catholic and wearisome that I just can't
be moved. I didn't know what to say. . .

Yesterday I didn't do anything sociable or journalistic; that is
to say, I did everything: I worked. Began a cycle of coloratura
songs with orchestra on Dryden poems for Miss Fleming. Today
I continued. . . At lunch there was Victor Grandpierre and a
beautiful Spanish painter named Ortiz. Went to the theater this
evening with Erlanger: Sartre's adaptation of Dumas' *Kean—*
a confused virtuoso solo for the miraculous Pierre Brasseur.
Opening night and hoarse voices.

Now tomorrow once again I won't have time for any creative
work (but still we can't retire into the country and live among
the bees and beasts as though they were like us). Because lush
Lise Deharme is coming to lunch. Afterwards I must get the
invitations printed for our music party here next month; then I
must buy gloves and socks, and go to Galliani's for the complete
Dryden; then American Express for overdue packages, and
Durand's for manuscript paper; then visit Pierre Noël and bawl
him out for not giving my sonata more publicity; then kill an
hour *en ville* before going to the Quai Voltaire to pick up Gold
and Fizdale, who phoned me this morning to say they're in town
and with whom I have a date to dine; then meet Henri *aux
Deux Maggots* at ten; then return to take a bath (I average three
baths every two weeks, and the same number of letters home in

the same amount of time). So the day is shot. And having written it all down beforehand, I dread the repetition in reality tomorrow. . .

🌱

Who, nervous and unaccompanied at a cocktail party, does not think of *Four Saints in Three Acts*: "Saint Teresa seated and not surrounded."?

🌱

Vertès came to lunch, and afterwards I went to his exhibit avenue Kléber, but was too shy to enter, seeing so many people inside. His *vernissage* was the same day as Braque's and Nora Auric's: nobody was at Braque's but five hundred Very Important People were at Nora's. The celebrity of the Auric couple has overstepped their *valeur*, but they attend to their publicity with tireless persistence. At least this is the opinion of Marie Laure who quotes Cocteau: *"Ils ont l'âme chaussée par Raöul."*

🌱

And I shall always worship Eva Gauthier, if only because she once said (typical of her misinformation) to a pupil who was about to study Fauré's *La Prison*: "Now this song is on a poem of Verlaine which he wrote in jail where he had been put for cutting off van Gogh's ear."

🌱

Poulenc's music is adroit, clean and powdered, *dépouillée* yet expressive, economic and religious, careful, witty, uninhibited and schmaltzy. Yet he bites his fingernails dirtily and to the bone.

🌱

There is a story from Trieste of a drunk who mistook his wife's canary for a lemon and put it in the squeezer.

Now what do you think of that! In this morning's mail Mother forwards me the clipping of Paul Hume's column in the *Washington Post* entirely devoted to me and my *Corinthians*, which it seems Paul Callaway performed two weeks ago in the Cathedral with a choir of men and boys. (I never dreamed I'd have both those men and boys written about on the boat December 30th a year ago!) Where did my oldest friend Paul Callaway get copies of this recently completed, unperformed, and already forgotten piece of mine? *N'importe!* Hume is in agreement with me when he says that though my anthem is perfect he doesn't know whether he likes it. With Margaret Truman he was more definite.

Reviews of my music have never taught me a thing. They are basically useless, and form opinions (*after* the fact) for those who have none. Therefore I like to receive only good reviews.

When the curtain goes up on a Balanchine ballet, it is as though the eyelid of an entire public finally opened to the truth. There is no *need* here to "understand."

Could this be a love story if a Peeping Tom follows a loving couple into a fairground and onto the Ferris Wheel? The Peeping Tom takes the seat behind the loving couple, the wheel begins to turn. Reaching the top he begins to descend, the couple already lower before him. He stands, extends his arms, falls, smashing his chin against the back of the couple's suspended seat, drops to the ground, dies. Can this be a love story?

Julien has an unpublished tale about a man who is killed

crossing the street, while preoccupied with watching a beautiful boy pass by on the sidewalk.

❧

For John Latouche's marriage Virgil wrote a prelude and postlude for organ called *"In"* and *"Out."* When asked, he answered: "What's a wedding!"

❧

In reconsidering Poulenc's *Carmèlites* I hear it as a *chef-d'oeuvre manqué*. For, moving though the music is, the scenario itself concerns fear, which the opera does not.

❧

Art, sorrow, and beauty are perhaps useless, but no more so than earth itself. What is useful? Useful for what?

❧

Rørhjem was our original name. In Norwegian it means "mixed home," but was shortened, as they all were, by immigration authorities—oh, a hundred years ago. Rorem in Latin means "dew." *Et rorem misericordiae tuae perennem infundas* (and shed upon them the dew of your mercy).

❧

The prehistoric Henri Bernstein vanished here all normally, but Reeves McCullers committed suicide last week. . . Truman Capote is in Paris for a month now, going to funerals and aged since I saw him last, four years ago: smaller than ever yet smart, sterile, and scary. I like him. His books bring me more comfort than his presence though. He should learn not to monopolize in the parlor with his special whimsy, for he's no philosopher but a poet; no Cocteau but a court jester. He lives

fancilly in fear on the rue St. Honoré, and says unpleasant
things about people which others laugh at without wanting
to. . .

Old Satie to a friend: *"C'est sans doute parce que vous êtes
encore jeune que votre musique est un peu triste."*

I spent the evening, rue Christine, with Alice Toklas (whom
I'd never known, except for two seconds, years ago, at Nathalie
Barney's) because I needed information about Stein's copyright,
etc. And she is small and old as a unicorn flying through the sad
old-fashioned smoke of other autumns; deaf, with Virgil's style
and accent, quick as a whip. She seemed lonely in the endless
suite of rooms filled with unframed masterpieces and electric
heaters; and I had the impression she didn't want me to go.
As I was leaving I noticed for the first time by the door three
small and marvelous Picassos. Miss Toklas: "Gertrude always
used to say that if the house were burning down and she could
only take one picture, it would be those three!"

For a month the weather has been all balmy and soaked in
sunlight, certainly rare for a Paris autumn, especially when
night falls at four. The French reaction to this good weather is
of course suspicious: as soon as something doesn't go according
to tradition the French suspect the worst—in this case it's radio-
activity. And at the florist's window, rue du Boccador, there
are orange roses on display, real *orange* roses!

Tomorrow is the luxurious evening that Marie Laure is
sweetly giving for my songs with la Lescot for three hundred
unmusical people. A house is not a hall and I am nervous in
candlelight. Day after tomorrow it will be over. I'll get drunk

with Heddy then, it's already planned. Monday I could logically be in dead crumbs from a fray like Poe.

Meanwhile I work: the coloratura tunes—and a love-story for two pianos and two voices.

For an hour I've sat contemplating how the ball-point has formed the "*d*" in this sentence's final word.

Others die. But Lucian Freud has just married and we are glad for him.

Sometimes I've been able to consider excess as purification: to vomit is to cleanse. I've spent a third of my life in sleep, a third in drink, a third vomiting. After the music on Saturday I became drunk before three hundred people who had come to hear me play, and later went to the Pergola and Les Halles with Jean Stein in her Dior dress, getting our fortune told by a young man in lipstick. Awoke next afternoon at five, sticky from head to toe in the dried river of regurgitation which had smeared onto every object in the room with Protestant remorse. Then I began all over again, this time with Heddy, smoking hashish, swallowing *orthédrine* tablets, drinking beer into a state of numb stupidity. . . This is the first time in a year that I've drunk for days in a row, and I'm thirty now (I never used to be); it takes a week to recover from the pained muscles, dried organs, depression and hate. The ensuing sleep is difficult and spattered with dreams of insane-asylums, slaughterhouses, and statues fully clothed and fornicating all twisted. Today I have a certain dignity to preserve as a composer I suppose: if I died, five hundred more people than ten years ago would recognize my name in the paper; that's all.

Part 8
England, Germany and Italy: 1953 and 1954

Yes, I've been in London now for two days, asleep mostly, in its foreign mists, and staying at Terry McEwen's near Regents Park. The city is filled with Christmas trees, green and red store-lights, pink and white cupcakes, honest (I hate the word sincere) politeness, pigeons, and dears like Terry or Cecil Beaton or Jack Henderson, and bowler hats and hairdos with wavy shapelessness, and early dusk, and no night living. . .

Nightfall's at 4 P.M. and I've been in London for a week and a day. Henri went back to Paris yesterday from Victoria Station all huge and hidden like an elephant cemetery. . . During this time I've certainly done nothing yet worth changing continents for.

Wednesday: Lunch with Sonia Orwell, my favorite person in England, and perhaps my favorite *girl* in Europe. I tell her I've spent the afternoon at Buckingham Palace. She asks: "How were they?" (which could mean either the guardsmen or the royal family). Our entire conversation was of movie stars, the one subject that really interests me. The tragedy that television and easy voyages have made the flesh of the films a now-tangible thing, when in olden times our goddesses lived in the protective Valhalla of Hollywood. We hate the probability of Ava Gardner really going into the Flore like anyone else. . . Sonia tells me Cyril Connolly's latest *bon mot*: "I'm looking for a publisher who's more interested in literature than money, and who realizes I'm more interested in money than literature.". . . In the black of six o'clock I took a cab to Cecil Beaton's crimson interior at 8 Pelham Place. We spoke only of sex. He always seems sad, though I don't think he is, and makes me feel vulgarly American. He has a marvelous portrait by Bérard, and several small Francis Roses which are the first I've seen and better than I'd expected. At seven Ruth Gordon arrived with Garsin Kanin, and as I didn't know them I left, feeling depressed and envious before the camaraderie of theater folk who don't exist except in playful bitchy formal rapport with others, while a composer is necessarily alone (I'm shyer as I'm older, with a nuttier and more positive front, so that many people loathe me). . . Returning home to generous Terry's, I find two young authors: Mortecai Richler (with mistress) and Negro George Lamming (with wife); I could suspect that neither has far to go. Writers' mistresses are jollier with laymen than painters' mistresses: the latter (I've known them in hundreds from infancy) are all stringy-haired, testy, full of culture (which painters are not), unmusical but love folk songs, and eat out of cans. They generally paint a little themselves, yet hate all but their lovers' work.

Wednesday: Matinée of *Hansel and Gretel* at the Sadlers Wells with Andrew Porter. No work. Evening: went to see Muriel Smith at Drury Lane in *The King and I* and afterward brought her back to Terry's to eat and talk till 5 A.M. Muriel Smith, the first ever to sing my songs, *Doll's Boy*. Is it already ten years ago that I wandered with her on Sunday mornings in lower Manhattan?

Thursday: Lunch at Andrew Porter's. Weather shimmering and clear and un-British. Nervous and bored, as I always am with people who know more than I do about opera when it means less. To a creator, knowledge is unnecessary, sometimes even harmful. Funny how little I think about sex lately. Maybe it's just the English. However, they are immeasurably more gracious than the French; too bad they're less attractive. . . Christmas Eve and, bars in England closing at eleven, we went to an old Marx Brothers' movie, and at midnight Piccadilly Circus was an inferno; even in New York I've never seen such puking everywhere: screaming young gents in rouge and feathers beneath the closed eyes of the cops, despite Montagu; cold whores in bare feet; unexciting sailors ("*la solitude est leur royaume*"); a crowd around the taxi of bleeding cockney rape; all retching, snarling, laughing, all tight, all with English accents on this English night of Christ's birth.

Thursday: New Year's Eve. Saw *Madame Butterfly* for the first time since grammar school. Afterwards, gin-and-tonics until nine in the morning at the madhouse of Piccadilly and later at the weird party of a *couturier* named Bunny Rogers in a white lamé leotard and white flamingo plumes, who received two hundred glorious guests painted from eyelid to toenail in frog-green and hopping web-foot from room to room speaking liquory Latin, or gowned in red bishops' robes revealing the testicles, or in baby-bunting pajamas with a dagger plunged in the spine and smoking quietly.

Friday: Hangover. . . A calm French supper with James Pope-Hennessey who is nicer than anyone and who took me to the Fitzroy bar where we saw an ugly man: asking for beer and not alms was a Mongolian-idiot-type monster next to whom Boris Karloff resembled Lana Turner; his right eye was where his ear should be, the left cheek extended like a hump, on the tip of which was the other eye (closed), a full seven inches from his noseless face. In my hangover this Bosch-like creature made me faint, so that James and I had to walk to the Circus struck silent in the iced wind to buy toilet articles as gifts for Marie Laure.

Saturday morning: Markevitch rehearsal of *Coq d'or* at Covent Garden. . . Dead tired. . . Lunch tête-à-tête with John Lehmann *chez lui*. Talked of sex and the new "little mags": his own, *The London Magazine*; and Spender's *Encounter*. He thinks Eugene Walter is the only young American in Paris worth worrying about.

Early morning: Awfully ill, iller than ever these two weeks surrounded by my friends *les docteurs*. The hemorrhoids have been succeeded by *la grippe* and my breast is a tight lyre of snot—snot in tight wires. Nevertheless I must tonight take the sleeper to Munich; for partner I'll doubtless have *un viellard qui pète* and may die. Those who speak of their *aventures en chemin de fer* are liars.

Nuremberg: Still the silence of Germany which grows more penetrating after now two weeks, silence that gets louder. All I notice is their difference from the French, who seem superficial by contrast. If I'm lonely in this country it's because I see around me my own introverted Scandinavian-ness put to practice, not my attractive counterpart; the Germans behave as I feel, walking glumly with the gentile footsteps of my mentality. Perhaps I've never before seen myself, yet I'm not at home. Of course I know only Bavaria: how they love blackamoors, hunchbacks, dragons and clowns, but not (like the French) *le crime passionnel*. They're scrupulously clean—more than the French—and their cooking's as good as it's bad in England. Slow. Like Americans, they wear glasses. The women are colorless though the men are "not bad." Outrageous aesthetic sense: store windows contain a hodgepodge of the owners entire property, a mass of multi-colored sausages and lizard-skin radios sorted by a cyclone. At our concerts the audiences of even the smallest towns sit without a cough or paper-rattle, presumably loving music in general (with a thirst only for Lieder) yet hating themselves for hating our "modern" program. They applaud desultorily, without enthusiasm, that's how they are. Yet, if, as they think, they have a fine aural sense (unlike the French), they have no visual sense (which the French *do*). So Latins are visual, glib and dirty; Teutons aural, unsophisticated and clean.

The weather has been lovely and Heidelberg a cold dream, but what's all that without carnal delights (which, when we don't have them, we think all-important—though when we leave our dentist with one wisdom tooth less, we look about Union Square at the tramps and say silently and Germanicly: "You haven't been through what *I* just have") and when I haven't been in good health for a month. . . Here is the West's most senti-mental people who weep at concerts and who die of broken hearts; these same who invented concentration camps. Their contradictions tantalize but irritate their American keepers who feel (with what appears a minimal penetration) that if they *are* rather sorry for Hitler, they regret much more having lost the war. Five minutes after meeting Herbert List he told me with intimate pathos that he must leave for Hamburg soon to bid adieu to a dying mother. What could I reply? Then he showed me his collection of photographs. *Très troublantes.*

It's the epoch of what Bavarians call *Fasching* when these sober sunken-eyed sullen industrious beautiful bees let down their Catholic hair. I, too, went to celebrate, but what happens? I get drunk, am robbed without reward, and next night am questioned by a plain-clothes man at the station where I've gone to wander from sheer loneliness. Is *this* sentimental?

Later, long after midnight. Now I have seen Nuremberg and it is attractive, at least after winter-dark beyond the parapets which in warm times must flower with fruit. A kind of ironclad Florence. Roditi undoubtably knew the manners here more than I who, at the sight of what Henry James calls "the real thing," hide my head in a book. The bright, jolly Saturday streets this evening (brighter and jollier than Munich) brim with high Americans, quaint corners, moats, portcullises and such antiquities; the men all wear hats, gay sweaters and socks, Tyrolean feathers (and in summer, so I'm told, leather shorts to enhance the male muscles of their bicycle limbs), though the interiors are grim, and the ladies of the race are drab as ladybirds. Dammit, those night alleys are agile with beautiful waiters, and the beautiful waited while I, a fool, stay home writing a diary for fear of what they'd think (not knowing they don't think). . . The Pension Charlotte at 18 Klaragasse.

Still I've begun to *feel* this country, the side of it that converts call *gemütlich*. (In France I've never heard *savoir faire*, or *faux pas*, or *pièce de résistance* except by Americans; the French say *présence*, *gaffe*, *tour de force* or *plat de résistance*. Also their *music hall* is what we call *vaudeville*.) But I've had no true contact with any German. Last night we played at the Amerika Haus in Hof, but after each concert (before we can mingle with the audience and drink in the compliments any artist needs) we are whisked out of sight like foreign untouchables by the authorities.

Paris, I miss you like a Frenchman during the war, and at the same time how could you help but be changing for me?

Egk's music is a hash of reaction, yet during the war, and still, he's the toast of this land. When he says he likes my music how can I answer? Because he's in that school of *married* composers that bear only tedious children. He has quite fallen for my Chloë Owen, the constant presence of my provisional life, though as she is not *in* my life I can say little more except that she's a superior soprano. How many people really *in* my life do I ever speak of?

Germans. Their weak coffee. Their crucifixions show what I've never seen: the feet of Jesus quite puffed from the nails—which is what must have been the case.

Their lack of glamor. Yet they produced Dietrich, Hitler, Hildegarde Neff. Their lack of mirrors.

Their snowflakes the size of band-aids. Nuremberg: a décor on purpose, but the devastation is more than subduing. We Americans perceive a surrealist charm in balconies on wires attached to nothing, moats, church-shells and bomb echoes after ten years. But for the good Germans these landscapes are the artery of life, and the heart contains nothing but blood.

The audience is not permitted backstage afterwards; it waits outside to see us walk into the cold. But who are we? Nothing, compared to Neff or Hitler or Dietrich. They've never heard of us, but do want to say how they love music. We are touched more than they.

Freiburg: From my hotel window I look out (up) onto the Cathedral and down into the square which this morning is a market of improvised shops similar to those of Marrakech (and all German merchandising is deliciously snuggled into the flanks of the church since middle-aged times), with this Teuton sun of early spring that's been here since I came, beaming onto all, making happiness though I am a failure.

Weather dictates my humor more than love or work and in this country of Johannes Brahms (to whom Alvin Ross used to refer as "Yo Highness Browns") the welcome has by the gods been tender despite myself so that "I'm beginning to kind of like it," as Garbo said in *Anna Christie*. That day of snowflakes in Père Lachaise seems now as distant as the moon, as Paris actually is. Is not my golden trail through this country already spattered with the red of broken hearts although I'm about in middle-aged times? Although I see just other Ned Rorems in the street liking Latins more? For now we're willing to travel half-way around the world for a good lay, but then we saw through a glass darkly and having all took nothing, not knowing what we liked. Oh well, it requires a lot of time, and time out from music, and anonymity occurs only to the anonymous.

The German reaction to my music is impassive, but with the question: have you—do you sometimes—or will you ever write in the twelve-tone system? If not, why? At Darmstadt they say: "Which of the works on your program was twelve-tone?" I passed Wednesday morning with Hartmann (Wolfgang Amadeus) who was prepared to dislike my music in the event that it was not *sérielle*—plus the fact that he hates Americans. (I found him charming, fat, vivid, and quite receptive to my suggestion that he employ such "unknown" Americans as John Cage, Fizdale and Gold, Nell Tangeman.). . . When Stücken-schmidt writes in the July '52 *Musical Quarterly* that "it is precisely the syntheses attained in recent German composition that show that every stylistic freedom is possible within the twelve-tone technique," how then account for Hartmann's state-ment that this technique is the *only* one that eradicates national-ity and makes music universal—to contradict my remark that Nono's music is *malgré tout* quite Italian, and Stockhausen's quite German? So I amend my remark: if it's true this music is what he says, no matter from which country, that's because it all sounds essentially German. He laughs. Music is not a science of precision, but food for the soul (pardon the expression); not invention of sounds (which is only orchestration after all) but unalterable arrangements of tones made by a great man, relations of notes. Boulez has hypnotized Europe *à la* Hitler: even those who've never met him fear his charm. The force of a dictator (as of a saint) lies in the absence of personal libido; not *caring*, he can focus equally on everyone. Such a one in power is rare. So if Boulez (like McCarthy) were assassinated, a vanishing chaos would result, fertilizing the road of a genius whose ideas might be in absolute reverse. I can only say what I know, compose what I feel. Like everyone born in the twenties I have just discovered that today is yesterday's tomorrow and the velocity of living has quadrupled, hurling us—as invisible as cold cream—toward a death we thought would never come. Why keep a journal? It never records anything more stimulating than that in Venice one says: "Oh, but *you* should see the *pissotières* of Toulon," and once in Toulon you wish you were back in Venice to die like Wagner and Diaghilev and George Sand and Thomas Mann and the wings of the dove.

Later. The recital is over, Chloë in crimson and me in tails. No audience reaction: might as well play for the dying. Some nuns, and trains . . . trains . . . tomorrow we leave for Baden-Baden.

The disagreeable thing is to have been a child prodigy and then not to be anymore. I have seen the rise and fall of Hitler, of Shirley Temple; I heard the last concerts of Rachmaninoff and Paderewski. People are for the Young (and they are right) and I think of myself as young, but no longer receive prizes or adulation.

As long as six years ago Bill Bergsma said (at one of those Columbia get-togethers): "You and I, we're no longer the 'young composers'; there's a whole new generation that's succeeded us!" The only thing more somber than the feeling-sorry-for-oneself caused by a hangover is the one that comes in a perfectly clear head. I recall the Hauptmann-Lindberg kidnapping as well as this morning, yet Jean Stein was *born* that year. I'm no longer youngest, am often the oldest. I read of a songstress being groomed as "a *younger* Judy Garland"; but Judy was a child star younger than myself! What do they say of the music behind my back? Frailties, *démodé*, nothing at all (worse). For whom do grownups exist? Oh, I hate children and shall end up on the Funny Farm. Supposing I received tomorrow a five-thousand-dollar commission? I'm too lazy. Not too lazy to work twenty-four hours a day, but too lazy to make it *good;* I dread the admiration I so desire because I don't deserve it, and do. Mostly I fear the growth into being an established lesser composer. Yes I was spoiled by people I've now forgotten, who perhaps still exist, perhaps are still spoiling others younger, not envious that newborns breathe their air, and there's air for only so many. Already in 1945 Janet Fairbank wrote that I had a reputation as the most undependable lush in the music world—not winsome or glamorous as I'd imagined, just obnoxious. In Fez I showed the brothels to my dear Yvonne Loriod (who happens, at the moment, to be the toast of Germany—probably because she's strongly faithful to what she believes, which I'm not sure I am). There's a girl: but she was never young, so it's easy. Neither was Dietrich, and the two are indeed different. The chief of Amerika Haus tonight (dull and thirty-five) referred to "folks of *our* generation." His head is entirely gray.

I have crabs again! How do you say "Larkspur Lotion" in German?

During one of our long long train dialogues Chloë explained that although she liked to sing my songs better than anyone's, etc., they lacked "the virility of necessity," and I couldn't spend my life as the spoiled child. At this moment a waiter of the Speisewagen dropped a clashing platter, and though it was symbolic of nothing, I mention it for what it's worth. At fifteen I'd already written a novel. Virile. I've never been weak, have always known what I want. Do I today? I will not be dominated, but oh, I *will* be possessed. A two-piano team has not these worries: it's locked like Siamese twins who never go crazy. Now my head has fallen to my navel, limp as the Burmese lady's when the rings are removed from her neck. . . Grammar-school days when Jean Edwards and I sprinkled pepper from the balcony upon an audience in paroxysms below, or spit in the fudge we sold, or swung high on the rings in the silent gymnasium while excreting onto the floor. When I'm drunk and meet a child-time goddess (as I did Greta Keller last Saturday here in Munich) I can only blubber so that she wonders what I am. When sober I am caustic and say to pregnant suburban ladies who already have a child, "Ah, one and a half, I see!" though they don't think this funny. Andor Foldes comes to stand with us as we have our picture taken. . . Well, we'll do our last concert Friday with pomp and parties and then I guess I'll go to Rome—less for the beauty and music there than so as not to be forgotten as even Garbo cannot be when we see her glide nervous as a moth in that divine revival of *Grand Hotel* now circulating in Germany.

Pensione Rubens. Well, I've been in Rome nine days now . . . Mostly I came to see my beloved Maggy and for Nabokov's Contemporary Music Congress; now Maggy too has left (this time for Genoa and Spain) and the music will soon be ending, so Friday my plane flies to quiet Paris from where I've been absent as long as when in America a year and a half ago. What can be said but banalities of this city where it is a tragedy not to be in love?

Leontyne Price, beautiful in a gown of blue sequins, soprano-
ing by heart and tonally (after hours of villainous bearded
dodecaphonists), sang Sam Barber's *Hermit Songs* perfectly but
with a trace of Southern accent, Lou Harrison's Rapunzel aria
gorgeously but with a suggestion of Southern drawl, Sauguet's
La Voyante in elegant French but with a shadow of Southern
croon. Her success was so great that she was permitted an encore,
and performed an unaccompanied spiritual *with no accent at all!*

It's the *talking* about music I hate; the redundant café intelligence makes me sigh. Who wants to be smart in Rome? This
maze of concerts we've been attending has proved how little competition there is for beauty. It's shown too that old acquaintances
after the years have simply grayer hair. But what can we say for
Rome? The brightest love letter is banal. The whole thing's
been equalified (thanks to Chuck Turner, who arranged it)
by my meeting with the two French sadists who left me deliciously crippled in the apartment overlooking the Forum, and
went off into the night on their motorcycle.

Charles Henri Ford, now a photographer, takes my picture.
I tell him I want two kinds: some very *sincere,* some very
chichi. "But sweetie," he says with a blue-eyed Southern lisp,
"I don't know the difference!"

Broken German hearts. Letters from Germany tell what I've
always been told no matter how I change (since even the
brightest love letters are banal, etc.): that I play with hearts,
but a day will come, etc. when I'll have no more friends, etc.
If I could write a quartet as good as Elliott Carter's, I wouldn't
care. Meanwhile I'm really in love (and it's sad) with those
I sleep with, though ten minutes after I want to say, "Get out!
I've things to do," as the Roman summer comes through the

window. . . The writer Miserocchi told me too that when we met at Bestigui's in Venice '51 he'd left a note at the Danieli saying that since his young friend's suicide I was the only one who could give him the *goût de vivre*. I never answered and had forgotten. If we are good to all who love us, what is there left for ourselves? Rome, Rome. Each one says selfishly: "No one has loved you as I do.". . . Mostly I've liked the many meals with Peter Watson, the lots of lunches with Ben Weber.

The only diary history of any import is of tedious incidents which publicity weaves into scandal: Stravinsky was refused entrance to the opera (Henze's *Boulevard Solitude*) for not being in formal dress. A real fight ensued. As Bob Craft was with him and Ned Rorem standing by, they both got in the papers all over the world. That's all. But I *do* love to see my name in print, even in the phone book.

Chez Jacques de Préssac: Palazzo Massimo. My final Italian afternoon and I am alone. It is raining so hard and long that it looks as though the plane may not leave and there'll be another interminable anticlimactic wait, which is bad, for in myself I've already quit Rome. My books are packed so there's nothing to do but sit, and the rain goes on. The toilet drips nervously, I'm bored and sad; crowds in the wet streets; across the way is Tosca's church, and the rain, and the rain.

Part 9
Paris: 1954

Marie Laure's in the Midi, so I'm alone and frightened. So much work to do, at a loss as to where to begin; so much music to write, books to read, so much love; if I could just be like the Catholic and ambitionless Romans who have only to walk into the street to be convinced it's no longer worth the trouble to aspire towards greater greatness: the greatest beauty has been there about them for centuries; and they live as was meant: by love, not work.

Two years ago Jean Marais visited me in my high sunny back room at Hôtel des Saints-Pères. (The desk clerk below, agog, had announced by phone: *"Le Marais monte!"*) He peered at my personal patterns, appeared tearful and confused, and finally said, *"Mais vous n'avez pas l'air d'un compositeur."* Indeed most people—musicians even—*do* think composers are bearded or dead, and I came across so many throughout Germany who'd been singing my songs for years that I felt both dead and bearded, abstract. I myself never existed for them. Just my notes.

Learned at the Roman Festival that I have minimal competition, and have never been afraid to say what's on my musical mind: I don't avoid the question the way Ben Weber does when he obliges his ninth-chords into an atonal scheme.

When I have a hangover I go down to Marie Laure's yellow and green ceramic bathroom and fill the tub with emerald bubble-foam and two kinds of bath salts (pink and blue gifts from Patrick O'Higgens). Then I get in and when it's over I'm sprayed and smeared with *Rose* from Rochas, and come back upstairs for Lanolin and Russian Leather and carnation talcum powder, not to mention D.D.T. for crabs and a suppository for piles. And so to bed: smelling like heaven and looking like hell, awakening again with a clear-fuzzy head and a broken back.

❧

Last winter, just before leaving London, on a rainy day without much time, I said to Andrew Porter: "What kind of sight-seeing can we do for the next hour and a half?" "Well," he replied, "we could visit the tomb of Radcliffe Hall." And we did.

❧

More than a month since I have written in this journal, and I don't remember a thing of these forty days back from foreign lands except having drunk and drunk and drunk. Yes, the concerto was played gorgeously by Julius last Sunday on the Radiodiffusion, and Villa Lobos conducted the other half of the program. He says I'm the only young American he considers, etc. I am drunk again with flattery all about. But these awful moments when liquor assumes a proportion far greater than music, *oh là,* I get scared. It *is* hard to write music—and when it's written it runs so far away. Editors are mongers, all or most— and years ago (dying to see my work in print at any price) I signed away my most beautiful things to cheats, to criminals. . .

❧

Anecdote: A large crown on one of my back teeth feels unstable, but I forget about it. After a private concert *chez* Mme.

Verniaud last month I take my plate from the *buffet* and sit with Marya Freund (we all wrote songs last fall for her eightieth birthday). I bite into a sandwich and feel what I take to be a snail shell screech between my teeth. Unconsciously I remove the object which I place on the plate of Mme. Freund when her eyes are turned. Three minutes later, my tongue having found a huge hole, I yell, *"Mon Dieu, j'ai avalé ma couronne!"* and everyone comes running with advice: Eat this, drink that, so that it can go down and come out without injury to the intestines! I sit back, livid, resigned. Five minutes later Mme. Freund screams, *"Mais qu'ai-je donc là entre les dents?"* and they all come running back as she removes from her mouth my crown covered with spit and crab meat. Again I sit back, pale with humiliation and relief.

The artist himself is ignorant of the divinity working in him, he makes the music by inspiration and lives his life a pathetic blunderer; you take in the music greedily and turn on him in fury. You are disgusting; I bother to say it because I need your love and aid, you are the only society that there is.—PAUL GOODMAN, The Dead of Spring

I have dreamed of Boulez' approval as though I'd done something wrong to sing my songs as I do. Paris is stupidly aclamor about this "new" sonorous art, just as though I hadn't heard the same and better concerts fifteen years ago in the Middle East. Cocteau is also at the Marigny (having heard the word *Boulez* only that afternoon, and afraid of being left behind) shouting after the music is over, *"Mais le public, pourquoi il ne réagit pas?"*

A day like today all gorgeously sweaty in a summer sapphire sky makes me too exhilarated for work. I need to gain weight, though nothing is more gently sad than supping alone in a foreign city. Eugene Istomin is in Paris again and he on the contrary needs to stop eating. (Why are *all* pianists so obsessed with food? Singers need to use their mouths in all the ways—but why pianists?) He tells me that our Xénia whom I miss is staying with Anna Lou Kappell. Early last month in Rome, on seeing Aaron Copland again for the first time in years, we decided to go sup (gently sad in a foreign city) *tête-à-tête* on the tiny Piazza Mattei, and there he said that during the months after Willy's death he sensed a *relief* in Anna Lou; that Willy, being her greatest experience, was also her greatest strain; and now, even though crazy with grief and emptiness, she need never again make an effort. All death is relief, though it all makes us feel wrongly responsible; any end is sad. Back in '46 when I first met her in Tanglewood, Grace Cohen said I'd always have someone to look after me. And what's old-fashioned one place is brand new next door: Cocteau is considered hot stuff throughout Germany. Generations touch me! and I'm getting so old that I can see rises, falls. My own life and epoch of Blitzstein or Latouche; influence of Falla on Paul Bowles; the "thirties" which didn't exist in the forties (it was the "twenties"), but do now, etc.

While my fever was on and I lay in bed the friends came visiting, Patrick Burkhardt nicely brought a basket of too-red strawberries, and as I ate them (sitting in my bathrobe of strawberry-colored terry cloth and looking pretty because of the flush thermometers give to the very ill) he said they should be offered by cupids flying about my face. Out of the chestnut foam of my scalp, I quite agree, and the sensation of nails in my ex-tonsils. I did not know what Americans were before I came to Europe. The beauty of fever. In America I never knew the appeal of Americans, being one there myself.

Garland Wilson, the Negro pianist at the *Boeuf sur le Toit,* expired down in the rest-rooms there this week after vomiting four quarts of blood. It's said his liver burst from overdrinking . . . And Roditi told me that my old puppeteer Frank Urbansky died of liquor two months ago (good Frank, who once related how, at an Alcoholics Anonymous meeting when all the members were grimly discussing the insurmountable difficulties of small problems like getting laundry done when one is tight, he simply said, "Don't worry, it'll all come out in the wash!"—which the A.A.'s didn't think funny). I can't help finding these deaths ominous, though doubtless I'm still not feeling so well. I get more frightened, more ashamed; ashamed of nudity. But isn't drunkness archnudity? The will power of a fern.

Old people, like babies, all look alike; time and art are fevers of the young.

But I'm not winning any thinking contests (no "heavy thinker," as Eudora Welty says) so I'd better go to bed as anyway it's late and I'm trailing ill. Tomorrow I'll have happier thoughts.

Rain, without cease, rain. For weeks it's been cold as November. Cocteau seems really dying this time (he's installed just across the square *chez* Mme. Weissweiller). Spent my last money on new clothes Thursday; Friday I immediately had the jacket stolen by an Arab in Les Halles. All day long I play and replay Kurt Weill's masterpiece *Der Jasager* on the piano, without understanding a word of the German about the child-student who kills himself. With my hang-over Saturday talked long of this to Sauguet dining at St. Germain with Guy (who was in town for exams), and also Jean Bertrand and Jacques Dupont. Jacques has exhibited my rainy-pink-and-lavender-sly portrait of three years ago in his show, and it's already bought by Marie Blanche.

In the cold of last evening I went to see dear Jean Leuvrais' outdoor production of *Bérénice* in the Cour de Rohan, with François Valéry who had phoned because I owed him money. Now for five years I have never particularly "dug" François, basing my opinion less on our "hello" acquaintance than on his rather cowering manner. But as is sometimes the case he turned out to be *sympathique* after hours alone during which we returned on foot through this mysterious summer-cold from those marvels of the *troisième arrondissement* along the Seine to the rue de Renne where we had supper and talked of all things until three in the morning. Of course his main interest for us is personal news of his dead father with whose works he nevertheless seems to be less familiar than other cultivated Frenchmen, which is not surprising in that most sons of the famous recoil from their parents' output in an effort to become individuals on their own. All the same I was distressed when he couldn't identify a quotation whose source I questioned. (Paul Bowles uses it in *The Sheltering Sky*: "The dying man looks at himself in the mirror and says, 'We won't be seeing each other any more.'")

> *Hell gave me my semi-talents. Heaven*
> *gives man a whole talent or none at all.*
> —HEINRICH VON KLEIST

The most discouraging thing I can conceive is that people should say, on hearing of my death: "It's too bad he didn't leave a masterpiece, to make his disappearance a tragedy instead of a farce."

No matter who you are you can't know Death's significance before thirty because it's a cumulative experience. I went to see Julien Green and we sat once more face to face in his "Vermont room," and had nothing to say to each other. That's being thirty and knowing change and death.

The twelve-toners behave as if music should be seen and not heard.

If you wish to raise your children well, treat them as though they were drunk.

If I—when we—remain jealously home at night, our loved ones out fornicating, how much more aching is the dying man's gaze from the hospital window to one walking by and vanishing into a vital tomorrow!

More and more, passionlessly, I don't, in the large sense, *care*. Yet doesn't this diary, paradoxically by its very being, show that I *do*?. . . And every day I am aware of growing older, not only in years and attitude, but in relation to the young who, with their inherent assurance and voracious inhaling, push me from the scene as a mother pig crushes a runt.

> *What can be said at all, can be clearly*
> *said; of that which eludes utterance, best*
> *say nothing.* —WITTGENSTEIN

Reworded, the above makes music's definition. Because the astutest utterances *about* music (from Sappho to Suzanne

Langer) are meaningless to someone who's never heard any. Music defines itself.

Last week Poulenc invited me for our bimonthly *tête-à-tête chez lui* so that we could play what we've each been writing, and drink some dubious-tasting lemon tea which the middle-aged French take for their *crises de foie*. Francis (*qui me tutoie* and who calls me *mon enfant*) never fails to amaze me when he speaks of how magnificent his own music is. It wouldn't occur to *me* to speak of my particular musical tricks or miracles for fear of boring people, yet I readily talk of how luscious my *skin* is. . . He was in a typical swoon over my choral songs *From an Unknown Past* and, preferring it to my piano concerto, thinks *le choeur* is my principal talent. I of course return the compliment—particularly as regards his heavenly *Stabat Mater*—loving to enchant the man who has all the enchantment and instinct of his country and who needs none of the intellect of his colleagues to protect his talent.

I have committed only one pointless crime (Gide's *acte gratuit*). When I was seven my old ill grandmother—full of love for me—was naked in her bath as we laughed and talked together. Suddenly, when she wasn't looking, I threw a glass of ice water on her. In her terror her false teeth fell out, and she began to weep without defense. I fled.

Why have I only a lovely souvenir of Morocco? Because in spite of its certain uglinesses I have never been drunk there.

Since tomorrow I must leave Paris for a summer of work in the Midi, this whole evening was spent alone, covering the city on foot looking for love which (perhaps because of nearsighted-ness) I did not see, or at least did not recognize, or did not admit that I recognized. But it's the best way of becoming intimately acquainted with a town, and special maps should be made of lovers' lanes the world over for the tourist in a hurry.

Returned to see the Tchelitchew exhibit. Pavlik (who knew me when I was what he calls a little boy) gave me a nervous lecture on the evils of drink: the creator spirit is too beautiful and rare for voluntary ill health and the artificial stupefaction of drugs which have never aided artists, but only (he quotes Tolstoy) "smothered the requirements of their consciousness.". . . Of course I've heard this argument inside-out a thousand times, but it gives me a start to be scolded by the artist in front of whose "Leopard Boy" I used to stand transfixed in the newness of New York and First Times.

Part 10

Hyères and Italy:

1954 and 1955

Il se pourrait que la vérité fût triste.
—RENAN

*J'ai le coeur et l'imagination tout rem-
plis de vous; je n'y puis penser sans
pleurer, et j'y pense toujours. . .*
—MADAME DE SÉVIGNÉ (in a letter to
her daughter, October 5, 1673)

Because now, after five years of European living, I know less
than ever what an American is. When *there*, being one, it never
occurred to me to question. Now I see them: understanding
less than anybody, am charmed.

It was while in Cannes for a few days last week with James
Lord and Jean Lagrolet that I met Bill Miller and realized more
than ever that I realized less than ever what Americans are,
especially those cultivated ones without occupation, winsomely
cruising the Continent more lost than the Jews. The secret of
translation is not in the aptitude for foreign tongues, but in
knowing your own language.

Summer loves. Ach! the wistfulness. How can wars teach us
anything since each child must make the same mistakes, birth
being always new, and no one's born wise?

A European can't know what a "camp" is.

All the French words, slang and medical, for the male members are feminine, and are masculine for the female.

Here, for my old age, is a chronological digest of the past six weeks or seven:

Before leaving Paris, Germaine Lubin spoke to me of her "friend Hitler," leaving me nothing to say. . . Gerard Souzay sang Golaud beautifully, and during the intermission Leda Fournier announced she'd had a *rêve équivoque* about me. So did André Dubois, and now he's become *préfet de police*. . . Cocteau nearly died of a rent heart after forty years of reflection on this organ. Poulenc too, so melancholy, feels death nearer, but it's imaginary. . . Agnès Capri dyed her hair red, and Florent Schmitt is more tediously reactionary than ever. Alexis de Rédé gave a party and I went. I like George Chavchavadze and he's a friend. Little Jean Stein loves me. From a taxi I saw, on the corner of rue St. Dominique, a fruit-seller who had no face, bombed—and lunched with Florence Kimball who seems to like *la foire*. That's all. In Paris. Silly to have noted it.

Since I've been in Hyères there's a steady flow of passers, with the regulars (particularly Oscar) behaving as dubiously as ever while a year older, and it's my fourth summer in this south.

I've been reading quite a bit: Petronius, Isherwood, Mauriac, Musset (in preparation for the Sauguet opera in Aix which turned out to be lukewarm), Maupassant, Balzac, Ray Bradbury, Christopher Fry (whom I never like), James (as usual), Apollinaire's biography, B. Constant (*Adolphe*), the proofs of James Lord's novel—and am studying Italian alone just because I guess I am in love with someone in Pavia.

The "semiregulars" *à demeure* (other than Oscar) have been to date: Robert Veyron-Lacroix (more sympathetic than ever, with whom I play four-hand Bizet at nightfall); the Auric's and *entourage* next door (Georges before supper intoxicates us daily, and then the supper with cider is divine); Dora Maar; Arturo Lopez and his followers (*pour moi une bande inconvenante*); Louis Ducreux and Michel de Ré; a party for the gang who came to play Gide's *Saül* on the church steps; Denise Bourdet (we're buddies now) and Jacques Février (it's incredible how badly the French play their own music); Lily Pastré with *her* infant Boris Kochno; Milorad Miskovitch pretty as can be; Tony Gondarillas (old in his hill); the Godebski clan; and Diana C. disguised as a scarecrow. Also Claus Bulow.

Am beginning a requiem on modern poets (compiled by Paul in *The Dead of Spring*), and maybe an opera on James Lord's *The Boy Who Wrote No*. Receiving suicidal letters from Jerry Ackermann, and looking with wonder at photos of the Hamburg suicide of an adolescent torn to shreds in the lions' cage. Spent a night in Toulon with an Armenian met in Aix, the hotel surrounded by yelling whores, from whom (the Armenian) I've been receiving packages of oriental pastry ever since. Citizens of small countries are more consciously proud of what they are than big-country citizens. . . In Aix, Marcel Schneider finally made me a translation of Weill's school-opera *Der Jasager* which for two months was the only music I liked. . . Seeing movies, endless talking, manufacturing logic, reading Jünger, writing letters, worrying about money, eating well, seeing a lot of Philippe Erlanger, fiery or dull evenings in St. Tropez, long talks with Denise not only on death and the present sense of miracles, but about women who copulate with dogs and get stuck and are humiliatingly obliged to call the doctor, etc.

All of which stupidly brings me past a circle of seniors whom I perhaps wrongly overfrequent back to the trials of this minute which now seems empty since nothing exists in the present except an orgasm or a broken heart, neither of which I have. (The writing of music is not of the present, it is of a domain that has nothing to do with time.)

Yet with my elders in this my sixth foreign summer I've still had seasonal idylls. In Europe I've been twice in love, three or four times almost in love, five or six additional times (additional people that is) not quite almost in love; one, or two (or three) hundred one-night stands (does one count such things anymore? if we were accurate we'd find ourselves far shy of the mark) which is inferior to the American score, if it matters; one or two hundred people in love with me, and this is the most important: it is greater to be loved than to love, it implies far more. . .

Well, the reason I'm learning Italian since three days ago is because last week in Cannes I met someone who works in a *magazzino d'alimentazione* in the outskirts of Pavia (the Armenian works in a *magasin d'alimentation* in the outskirts of Marseilles), about whom I brood incessantly with that pleasant nausea that comes at the beginnings of love; and though it is a sheer invention that may never be of use, for the instant it's as precious as a beating blue heart in a crystal box. A feeling that makes us wish to say: I love you, so leave the room that I may suffer your absence agreeably, knowing you'll be back before the evening meal still with sea-salt to be licked from you; so leave now, I'm impatient for you to leave (though I only met you yesterday) that I may tell friends how happy I am; leave, so that expectancy for your return may be stronger than your return; or leave forever so that I may write you and suffer the only pleasant pangs that have any meaning, that make a difference; so that I may learn Italian and come maybe next month with joy to visit you and be disappointed because love was not designed for nourishment by the unfocusing imagination of absence, but meant for immediate consumption, and now it's too late; because, even though you might be better, you're not the same as I remembered. . . None of which keeps me now from hours of practice at learning to say in Italian such useful things as: "Where are the monks? Are they in the refectory?" I'm glad to know that nothing, nothing will ever ever kill the capacity for wanting to fall in love, even when the object seems ridiculous or impractical, or when work grows hollow during such meditations.

❦

In Cannes again. It's six-thirty in the afternoon. I'm feeling low. This is a town invented for pleasure, where one has no right to depression, where one must bed with as many as possible in the shortest space, where I'm useless and forgotten, thinking on Pavia (I've had no letter) with that stifling empty choked screaming desperate ill sleepless sensation that comes to persons in love, no matter who. No matter who you are, a sick heart is a sick heart. The choice of lover is one's own business, but if you're Beethoven in love with a hat-check girl, or a hat-check girl in love with Beethoven, or Tristan, or Juliet, or Aschenbach, or the soldier on furlough, the suffering is equally intense and its expression just as banal. Helpful friends saying "It's not worth it!" are of no help; logic does not enter this domain of helplessness. So here I am dumbly in Cannes again where the remembered cobblestones of any alley appear yelling for help— all this for someone in Pavia who "isn't worth it.". . . These words are as commonplace as all others in love, but maybe they aid me a little. Each morning when I wake up I say today I'll think a little bit less about it, and if I eke out a bit of not-so-good work all goes well for awhile, *mais vient cet horrible cafard d'entre-chien-et-loup* and I'm reduced to the state of wasteful reflection that makes fools of greater than I.

Then what have I done *pour soulâger* my long hangover (because I got falling-down drunk here Saturday with Robert Veyron-Lacroix)? Only the sordid encounters: it can't be believed, I want to cry. There's a club called the Casanova where a kind of man dressed as a kind of woman looking like a giant squid in drag, sings Auric's famous waltz; today I had lunch with George Bemberg after all these years and we spoke of the music we've always loved in common (Debussy's *Dieu qui l'a fait bon regarder*, etc.); afterwards in the afternoon I went for a rocky wet ride in the motorboat of P. le B., a lawyer vaguely Communist I guess and so forth. But none of these is *the* person, no words help, all the brains and blood of the solar system don't mend the unmendable. So I dragged myself back alone along the *croisette* to the hotel, and here I am now.

In Cannes' harbor two second-rate yachts owned by Yankee gents bang together. Nine-tenths of what we speak think and write isn't worth the trouble—including this sentence. The other tenth? Not worth the trouble either.

The kind of remorse I feel after drinking or after love-making (though the first is a filthifier, the second a purifier) is of course strictly Quaker. For instance, I'm ripped with shame at returning the next night, the next year, to a place where I may have disgraced myself in a *déchâinement* of stupor; whereas our painter Jacques Dupont, a Catholic in a Catholic country, declares that nothing *we* can do is "wrong," and he suffers even physically less than I the next day since it doesn't occur to him to have a conscience. Oh, Protestants sure made me real passive.

> *One must be really brave to choose*
> *love or writing as one's guides, because*
> *they may lead one to the space in which*
> *the meaning of our life is hidden—and*
> *who can say that this space may not be*
> *the land of death?*
> —DEMETRIOS CAPETANAKIS

And Colette too has died these days.

James in such stories as "The Great Good Place" or "The Jolly Corner" has taken us into realms that are not concerned with death and life, yet he died all the same. These authors, those routes in time, with what we call the future which is just a series of static landmarks we approach and pass (since tomorrow already exists, why can't we sometimes reach it quicker?). Still they die anyway; our deaths are there waiting. . . I have always kept a yearbook of appointments. I need only to refer to a given date in, say, 1947, to see what I was doing that day. Now, if it were possible to buy the engagement pads to be used from today until the end, the pile wouldn't be so high. Generously I'd need forty-six books between now and the year 2000, and I've already passed the lunch-period of my life.

Pavia (Albergo Moderno): A hangover can be transported from Marseille to Stockholm! You have only to get drunk and next day board a plane, getting off six hours later in a new country: a different language, but the same hangover. Loving hearts too can be carried about without harm, and, as Maggy used to say: "A good lay is worth going halfway around the world for" (to which Norris Embry used to add: "But I've *been* halfway around the world!"), which is exactly why I am in Pavia today and don't regret it. The tourist is truant here, and as I seem to be the only one I peer among the buzz of honest work feeling much as I did years ago when I'd ditched school, and having then nothing to do felt guilty at the sight of a bricklayer.

During the past three weeks in Hyères I spent two hours a day learning Italian alone in preparation for the magic Saturday when not three minutes after we'd met in the Milanese airport P. had slipped the gift of a gold medalion around my Quaker neck. Oh, the grown-up French and Swedes and Germans and English never were children, but Americans and Italians always stay so, and thank God I learned this language a little, for in Italy they go right to the point.

Today I will leave Pavia, go by motorcycle to Voghera which is cheaper, and nearer P.'s home-town of Dorno. Each tiny city in North Italy is sadder than the next, but this people has a different level of perception than the American and the poorest shepherd sports an enthusiastic heart. I've lost all sense of place, and being addressless, no "outside tie" could contact me. Am dominated by this impossible situation of love and no longer think of music. P., eyes all naïve, is excited by an article on me in the Milanese *Derby* which appeared coincidentally with my arrival in Italy Saturday. P. was born a twin and will live and die in poverty in that gloomy unheard-of village with a great heart, dear arms, animated ways, and preoccupation with what we ambitious ones name the "simple pleasures." Why are these worlds such oceans apart? Yet it is just the primary distances that make our chests bloom impossibly. I cannot live here forever as though I were like them, without those facilities which are myself. But then where *can* I live?

Voghera: Shorter days, a small town, a season is ending. After only twenty-four hours everybody knows me already as the stranger, and looks askance at my sloppy dress, the bleached streaks of my hair. The humblest Italian has more *chic* than the richest German.

It is six o'clock in the afternoon and hot. What a troubled summer it's been, the season speeding past like the wind of foul television seen here from my hotel window smothering the modern streets of this distant town. It is Thursday. Tomorrow P. will not come over from Dorno to see me because the day must be spent killing pigs. Maybe half my life is over. Saturday I leave alone for Venice, the city of death. I could kill myself from the tenderness that chokes even my impotence.

Yesterday we passed in the Chartreuse of Pavia, the land's most luxuriant sepulcher with its hot gardens. But would I have found it beautiful had I been alone? Afterwards we went to the church of San Michele where once more I was ready to die.

Garbo in this language means grace (*con garbo—avec grâce*).
When I am a hundred P. will be ninety-nine. Our centuries
will always be different. Americans, Italians. . . I was not ready
to die.

The whole night long I cried, and again this morning. The
strength of an Italian peasant family which I, as a rich creator,
cannot combat. Even now that I have made this incredible
déplacement dans le bled we're still able to meet for only two
to three hours in the evening when P. should be sleeping, for
the daily chores are far from here and P. gets up at 4 A.M. under
the continual supervising eye of the ferocious *madre latina,* and
the families of southern Europe are indissoluable or they would
simply perish. These two or three hours then are pain to me and
the other twenty-two or twenty-one I use up in crying. There
is no piano here (I wouldn't play one if there were) and the
city's without interest, dreary as any small town on earth (not
unlike my childhood's South Dakota), where the foreigner can
be only the intruder. This afternoon, with Gianni, P.'s sidekick
who runs a haberdashery next to my hotel, to kill time (before
my projected excursion into the wee weird town of Dorno
tonight "to meet the family") I went swimming at the new
glossy pool of which Voghera is proud. As I was moping at
the water's edge reflecting in terms of tears and considering this
scarily banal vicinity and how love can awe the vocal cords and
cause a desire to die, as I moped, suddenly a loud-speaker, silent
until now, beaming on our drops, without preliminary introduc-
tion began to emit the quieter piano music of Satie. Of all
things! all times! places! All the music of my babyhood and I
was overcome. What's more, the pianist turned out to be
Poulenc, Poulenc's recorded fingers trickling out onto the ugly
piscina of a town he's never heard of, while he himself lies
delirious in Lausanne. Oh don't die friends, friends don't die.

I want you always near, am in love, and miserable. We, we are in love. Don't, friends, die. . . Perhaps I will never come back here again . . . it is easy to say. Now that my French is as good as English I don't want it anymore. I don't want music, I don't want the poems of Capetanakis (at moments like this the Bible, the solutions of poets don't hold up), don't care if Gold and Fizdale never play my pleasant piece with the voices they've not acknowledged, don't want good weather. I want you.

❧

After a strenuous week in Venice where curiously the first people I saw (the sustenance of my stay) were Fizdale and Gold (with Jimmy Schuyler), I am now again, by contrast, in Pavia with much the same frame of mind as before except that meantime Derain has died, and I have not had a real bath since leaving Hyères eighteen days ago. This time my hotel, l'Albergo Corso, is across from the Monarchist headquarters, though the Communist headquarters are in a classier neighborhood. I arrived here Saturday night.

Next day (the second of autumn). I'm writing this because I have nothing else to do. It's grown cold and tomorrow I go back into France, back to Hyères first and the comforting of Marie Laure and strange contrasts. Then up to Paris for three months of work (finish the Third Piano Sonata, orchestrate the Christmas Choruses and coloratura songs; write a piece for flute, and a Pindarian Hymn for Nadia's contest). I'll be having another birthday too, oddly enough, and at the beginning of the year I'll *not* go to America but to Rome instead forever if I can find P. a job there and a way of living for myself, no matter how humble.

Of course all this is merely words and words, when really my one wish is to say I love you I love you and it wouldn't be the first diary filled with useless information, though really, like the changing weather the changes of the heart make about the sole subject worth discussing. It could never occur to me here now that a war or shift of fortune might arrive to disturb all this. I am in love and possessed and shorn of personality. Every time's the first time—thank God for that! and that I have no pride in such affairs. And every time I say where was I and how have I lived till now though when it's over nothing can be more over and the possibility of resumption is less adequate than rape after orgasm. Meanwhile I spend my afternoons watching Pavia's cinemascope where during the intermissions even here we can listen to Johnny Ray exercise his contagious neuroses at throat-ripping velocity. Then after *How To Marry A Millionaire* I come out again into the reality of Pavian light (which to me is not so real) and wait, and wait.

Just now in Venice my first boss Virgil Thomson said in his dry Gertrudian style of this-is-how-it-is-and-there's-nothing-more-to-add: "Journals must be kept for their gossip value, since in any case the editor will cut all the sentimental parts." Also: "Come home now and start your career!" But I can't any longer base my living on other peoples'. If I choose to go to Rome and starve with someone poor from Dorno, while in New York without me swirls the sauce of people "getting ahead," it will be my choice, since this is the only life I know I have, and anyway I'll always write music. God told me to love. In Venice I saw David Diamond again too, about to have his fortieth birthday (I remember the screams on his thirtieth); he also has his life, nothing to do with mine; we have little to say. Why do I write all these excuses? Oh, I suppose it's just a Venetian report so that Virgil's "editors" won't cut.

On the evening of the ninth live pheasants pecked on the floor of the Fasani family's parlor in Dorno, the ugly town's dirt squares and limited life. The next day I stood in sweat on the train all the way to Venice where I arrived with a cold, sick and sad with love, left my stuff in the Albergo Paganelli and went onto the piazza to look for consolation and immediately bumped into Bobby and Arthur (whom I'd believed in U.S.) with whom I dined and had the first coherent conversation in a week because till then I'd been only blubbered in baby Italian. I spoke only of love. Next day came three magic letters from P. Spent the afternoon with Harold Norse who aggravates me; saw the new Chirico exhibit which is bad, and a thousand close friends in San Marco. In the evening Lenny Bernstein gave a concert with his new fiddle Serenade (built from Plato's *Dialogues*) played by Isaac Stern. Supped afterwards at the Taverna with Virgil and Mimi Pecci-Blunt, later Fulco. Everyone was the same only older, so I went home early to think about love and nurse my flu and be forlorn. . . Next day, Monday, saw Christina Thoresby who's helpful but boring because of her psychoanalysis and because she wants to be *dans le grand monde* but isn't the type, and who's a dear friend of Roditi, of all people! Spoke only of love. Then had lunch with Raffaello, lovable as ever with a new double chin, successfully *mondain* but only pretends to be helpful. I spoke only of my love affair, though he flattered me on my work and on everything else, and said that geographical tribulations help hearts, etc. Studied Italian some more. At four saw Miserocchi who's a pretentious bore and still an opportunist at sixty. At six-thirty had a lugubrious drink at the Bauer with D. again and we spoke mostly of my love. In the evening a dress rehearsal of Britten's new opera on *The Turn of the Screw* which I liked immensely, and even if it's not a masterpiece it's the piece of a master which Sauguet's opera in July was not. And there I met Bill Weaver, my pleasantest encounter. With him next day, Tuesday the 14th, I sight-saw: the Dali exhibit which disgusted me, particularly since afterwards we saw again that Carpaccio had done the same more rightly in the little church of San Giorgio degli Schiavoni which is maybe my favorite place in Venice.

Virgil made me get up at dawn Wednesday to go (with Efrem Kurtz) to a rehearsal of his flute concerto, a misty formless piece, elegantly played by Elaine Shaffer. The work is apparently a portrait of Roger Baker with whom we then lunched as Virgil pursued his sardonic advice. I am too thin. Haven't had a drop of alcohol in thirty-four days. Thursday, lunch at the Chavchavadze's (where it seems one *has lunch* in Venice) both of whom I like. Played the record of my piano concerto for young Philippe Entremont, George's protégé. At six Christina took Petrassi and me to Peggy Guggenheim's whose collection is the same as Marie Laure's only one-tenth as good. The Twentieth-Century Music Festival continues. In the evening attended the second performance of the Britten opera (which Virgil calls "The Screw of the Century") with Denise Bourdet and "drove" her home in a gondola to the Bestigui Palace. In Munich last winter Peter Pears had already warned me that the little girl's role would be taken by a lady-midget of forty. Of course it was a flop. Why not a boy dressed up as a girl? At those ages there is little difference!

The last two days in Venice were a composite of the other six: same heat and water, same people and wistfulness, same realization that I have nothing in common with those with whom I have everything in common: those agreeable Americans in Europe I can talk to on the same level of understanding, but understanding isn't *being* and so I came back here to Pavia by way of contrast as I said, and am sad and must leave tomorrow.

Here I don't know a soul; here is where I collect my thoughts and that is the bitter truth; here is where I wait.

Gropello is the gloomiest town! Father used to quote: "God made the country, Man made the city, and the Devil made the little town!" Gropello is formed of dirt, saliva, bare feet, and bathos. That is where P.'s brother works in a ceramic-factory all day long, where I was given three *échantillons* (not too pretty) to take to *La Viscomtessa*—as Marie Laure is called here. I was horribly touched; the monotony and resignation of poverty is so foreign to me; I am at a loss.

Our flaw is to reject what *is* precisely because it *is*. We *are,* we met, took root, so gently, but inconvenience obliges uprooting. New frail conveniences will waft or fling us to where we'll *be* again, replant seeds, leave them too to dry, to *un-be,* to fear, from fear. Life is inconvenient. It's not ego or evil but sheer mediocrity that's killing the planet.

Hyères: There is nothing I need write to help recall the drama of parting yesterday at the Milan airport. The first thing to greet me when I arrived back tired and ill in France was a message (in what seemed to me perfectly literate Italian) from P.'s mother saying she'd discovered and read all my letters and that if I wrote once more she would notify the police. Her note was dated the nineteenth. I can't believe that her police could be interested in a correspondence between two adults, though those letters reveal sensual penchants more frankly than this diary. In any case, were I in Italy, this *virago* could probably be embarrassing, and meanwhile she's demoralized me to a point where I neither eat nor breathe nor sleep nor work. Oscar and Marie Laure are as comforting as is possible, but these useless ironies in a short life are impediments. Consolation is that God has presented a trial of love, so I shall cope with it, dangerous patience, though I don't know where the sickening business will end. Here, too, is where I wait. I think I see the first wrinkles about the eyes, and my flesh responds like ginger ale at the thought of those hands I love. I too have a mother and love her still and left her long ago in a country of the present. We are all so different. And I am so tired.

Under my plate this evening James Lord compassionately slipped this verse: ". . . and human nature is not conceived to conform to human needs."

🌷

On dit que j'ai trente ans; mais si j'ai vécu trois minutes en une . . . n'ai-je pas quatre-vingt-dix ans?—BAUDELAIRE

🌷

Obstacles. They are, in a sense, the chief impulse (inspiration) for my every act and thought. And the long days fly past.

🌷

Some of me is gone and dead. Though I know these words don't have meaning, make any difference, when I read them later. It's a dreary September with the waiting days that drag by at a snail's pace. I've lost ten pounds, worry and smother, life's lowest month (which is saying plenty inasmuch as it's not yet accompanied by wine). I am in love and wonder at the reason of absence in this too-quick life-span. Nothing consoles, no book or speech or success. I'll be glad to return to Paris Friday after three months.

🌷

Rome, via Angelo Masina, 5B. Haven't written this diary in over three months: 104 days, to be exact. Not because I've been particularly happy (and diaries are for the schmaltzy moments) or even occupied with music, but simply because I haven't had time, with P. abandoning family, at my encouragement, to look for a job in Paris, then leaving Paris to settle here a month ago, coping with the unrest and scandal all this gave rise to. For if I live three lives I mix them together (wrongly perhaps) and don't keep problems to myself. Similar to Cuénod who, when I once observed, "But you pass with no transition from the subject of rough trade to Monteverdi as though they were the same thing," answered, "To me they *are* the same thing."

In the interim old Max Wald has died, my first composition

teacher, Chicago. Also Matisse, and our Jacques Fath. . . 1955, and is it already fifteen years (half of my life) ago that I was preparing to graduate from high school and had difficulty finding acceptance at a university because my grades were low? In the interim I received a commission from Louisville for whom I began *The Poets' Requiem,* and gave three concerts in Paris with my song in the mouths of Irma Kolassi and Miss F., the first a white jewel, the second a flop, though the orchestration of my coloratura tunes had the fragile sumptuousness of rope in ruby silk. I've hardly drunk; not that I've accomplished any the more for it (drinking was part of my rhythm), though I have more stamina to scratch in the knotty nest where I've voluntarily thrown myself. I've turned thirty-one. My craziest occasions were before twenty, but am I more balanced now that I recognize lack-of-balance?

Roses and zinnias: these are my favorite flowers. I am jealous even of your shoes, your sleep.

❦

Hairdressers, harpists, cooks: most are women, but the best are men.

❦

I have forgotten the hell-fire, the maniac, and dreams, my burnt letters. Alas, we can only be in love with those of our century. We should recall all: I can't wish even the most painful instants to have been wasteful.

Those are illusive (allusive?) words, I'm afraid. I grow lazy with the thirties. At least I have learned Italian.

What goes through the heads of parents reading their famous children's dirty books? Oh, the parents will do alright as long as the children are really famous and the books stay in print. But what goes through the heads of *friends* of parents when reading these Americans who so criticize their grownups? Just words

(illusive), the fools! Don't they know a symphony can be twice
as dirty? only nobody listens. . . I for one love both Father and
Mother tenderly and always have, though I realize the exception.

Let's get back to reality (the only thing which, by nature, we
should seek to avoid; its definition is different to each of us
although we must announce it as that which is *ugly* and should
be escaped from—artists sometimes succeed): there's been so
much of it these last three months! When I left Pavia to take
my plane back to Nice (September 23rd), from my taxi window
I spotted Peter Watson walking the dawn streets of Milan. So I
shouted, and we had breakfast. Now it's never strange to see
Peter in any city you accidentally happen to be in because he
travels (despite his money-complaints) into places where intelligent natures would expect consolation, and does it alone, hating
train-company and suspicious of love. I must not forget that the
evening of the morning I shouted my joy to Peter Watson in
Milan I was to receive the first of those letters (back in Hyères)
from P.'s mother. Others. Oh Mothers! Really this now all seems
so long ago it's a bore going through it again, and, as I say, in
my thirties I grow lazy. At least I know more today than yesterday what an Italian is; if this people has no sense of humor as
we know it (and as the French in a drier, bitchier fashion), it's
because they *are* a camp, it's a national characteristic, and you
can't be a camp within a camp.

Returned to Paris. How could my life *not* have seemed empty
(though Larry Adler asked me to write him a piece without
offering to pay) when only the uninitiated can believe that an
artist goes on being an artist when he doesn't have what he
desires? So that when P. arrived in France on my birthday I had
what I wanted (though the "friends" were against it), but suddenly found myself for the first time being *responsible* for someone, which I still am today in Rome where jobs don't grow on
trees.

I am now in the future. The present was love-time. Minutes

have assembled and built towards this moment. Wind seen from above. Our smallness, our bigness on earth. *The Poets' Requiem* opens with a quote from Kafka: "You can hold back from the suffering of this world. It is allowed. It is your disposition. But it may be that this very holding-back is the one evil you could have avoided."

❦

I am intolerant of those my age who retain faults I once had and vanquished—particularly the fault of timidity. Yet, as I advance, the more I grow afraid, really afraid, of everyone. Their indifference: a cruelty I've not understood, being myself inquisitive.

❦

P.'s gone now. An hour ago, for a long time to the North and a dying father. Another day of tears and tension unrelieved since August 8th. Back to that Pavian North for a death rattle in an *ambiance* of Catholic solidarity so foreign to me. (Are these the same Italians who astonish my tourist's eyes with their web of grafitti on holiest monuments? the same who produced the assassin Cannarozza—famous this week—who decapitated two ladies with a bomb in an Ancona cinema?) Yes, I am loved and in love and have never been so unhappy, with answerless questions, from a situation without solution. Is it worth it then to remain a month or four longer alone in Rome just to arrange a little concert at Mimi Pecci's or with Michel Chauveton to play my not-very-good fiddle sonata and not get paid, meanwhile not working and waiting and waiting for P.'s father to die, and then return to Rome where neither in spring will jobs be found, and always the money dwindles in spite of the three hundred dollars Miss Fleming mailed from New York? I'm getting to hate Rome, archeology where everywhere beauty smiles and smells of the dead, to hate Rome for all its warmth

where even January roses vomit out among broken pillars in the
Palatine, hate Rome (now all alone) in this good apartment at
35,000 lire with an out-of-tune piano on via Masina in the
shadow of that institute of mediocrity, the American Academy—
Rome, though in Paris with the animation there'd be the ice, and
also Howard Swanson sitting dark on a *tabouret* in the Reine
Blanche feeling sorry for himself. (Didn't I also, look at Gina
Lollobrigida two weeks ago sipping a soda at Greco's?) Though
I do not drink I have bad dreams which I try to forget though
they wish to be remembered.

But am I Job with this decision between love and ambition?
Looking about, I perceive not only that indifference ubiquitous
in each land, but personal plights as powerful and pathetic, and
the sculpture of Mme. Ibert representing a mother who cannot
help her child (we know her shock when her daughter lay dead
for days in an elevator shaft); or the joyful Poulenc now with
nerves and liver paralyzed, self-torturing in a Swiss hospital
where he writes saying (because his circulation is bad and stig-
mata appear on his skin): *"Au moyen-âge on vous brûlait pour
moins que ça!"* All this! Are we put on earth for such reactions?
such wars? our miraculous brothers who slumber in the muddiest
inertia too lazy to open their eyes? I've no more ideas, nor any
desire to save our world. . . On the walls in the crypt of the
Convento dei Capucini, decorated like a wedding cake in human
bones, are signs announcing that everything is vain save the
humiliation of worship. I am more sympathetic to Rome's poet
Penna who has given up versifying in favor of searching love in
Trastevere's regions. But he is born of the Catholics. While I
must continue writing music and remain alone.

By myself now in Rome and all by myself. Who'll do the
laundry and bring breakfast in bed? I have never really been
self-supporting nor do I feel this is necessarily a virtue. Today

I'm exiled, wading from room to room in tears up to my knees, having the solace of a few American friends: Kubly, who after all these years, lives again next door; and Bill Weaver with whom I go to the movies, and who's writing me a libretto. Afternoons I play my old songs to myself (like the heroine of a silent movie munching bonbons between sobs) and wonder how I could have written any of them previous to this affection's puzzle. "Slow, slow, fresh fount; keep time with my salt tears." Proving once more that creation, coming from within, is extraneous to outer lights, though this one of my nine lives began in August. I have always hated cats. I write songs on the eves of great meetings rather than later celebrating romance with music, just as my dreams anticipate actions instead of recounting them. At bedtime I try reading Italian: Pavese, Malaparte, Moravia (the pride of their country)—or the weekly film magazines which I prefer. As Virgil says: "Rome is the European center of the Catholic Church, the Communist Party, and the cinema industry." Movies are mine. Roman society is humorless and narcissistic; at best they imitate Parisians. I feel lonelier than Debussy at the Villa Medici sixty years ago. Those right and reasonable days of discovery when, at ten, I first heard his *L'Ile Joyeuse* where a new existence was revealed. Today all fails at my fingertips. The Hersent's visit brought me together with Vera Korène who projected a great sound of mine (as we dined at Passetto's) for *Les Mouches* of Sartre. Now this too is canceled as I'm not a French citizen. As for the Romans, not *one* of the elegant names it was suggested I contact (Barromeo, Caitani, Volpi, etc.) has seen fit to receive me; in their boredom it is only their loss. . . Would I feel better off in the mechanical rat-race of New York? or in Paris where H. L. De la Grange used to give parties so that I could play my tunes to Menotti? or once more in Germany where the people are too sentimental without the spontaneity of imagination, leading them far from individual decision? I am stupid about my medium, and especially Italian opera which doesn't interest me. Lenny Bernstein has become the rage of La Scala. No, I feel no wish to compose; am sterile, jealous, aging, cowed. I want only to love, and today this privilege is denied, I might even say by God. There is no place left where I am not a foreigner.

Hate again Rome and its imitation bright boys as at good Weaver's party all surrounding Visconti like Casals and Bayreuth or that God might even say by God—and I grew drunk and so dull, damaging those only possibilities. The almost-genius of Maria Callas was there too in a mink-gold dress. My work has long since ceased to interest me, nor do I any longer bother to bother; and once done it interests no one else nor even Maschia Predit with whom rehearsals are as difficult as teeth-pulling or borrowing money from the rich. Chester Kallman calls Auden "Miss Master." Miracles don't happen to me now. I wait, but they don't.

The hair of Iris Tree is still trimmed yellow in a china-poodle style. I never knew her in the February days of '49 when I did music to her play. Now she has here a teensy penthouse right on the Spanish Staircase and we're to write pop songs together for money-making. She lives with a pair of cageless doves, is completely daft. It was her birthday.

You are my leather and my honey, my yellow roses (like those in the Spanish Place), my electric chair, my drum, drill, sweat, and my thistle. I love you. Floods in Paris, and weeks of twenty-below-zero in Chicago. Now a new war in Formosa. Is it really five years back that Korea made me mute, that I wrote another

string quartet? I cannot read. My other starvation for books has
all evaporated and I do not want to look again to see said better
what is it all about. I prefer unable to sleep in the love rain and
dying to ask what is it and receive my own less complicated more
complex retort. How long could it all go on? Could we feel
otherwise than that this time you are leading me smack to de-
struction in involition and whimpering? If I should die now here
(I cry as I write it and it must be known), all that I have, money
and music and trinkets and hair, is left for: P. F., via M—— 13,
Dorno (Pavia), Italy.

❦

Empty and depressed, depressed and empty, over and over
again, that's all, for the same reasons general and private, waiting
for a footstep, sterile disinterest in work, lonesome for Paris
whose any ash-can is to me beautiful; lonesome most for you
(for all words starting with "P") whose any geography I'd disappear to always. Families, money, distances, these make me
empty, depressed. Maschia Predit didn't work out; empty things
to do. This afternoon I'm off to see Petrassi again with a musical
briefcase under my arm; unless he's very encouraging I'll return
to Paris in two weeks, stopping in Milan to see *La Sonnambula*
and try to put coherence into my love and my enemy Pavia.
Tonight I am to dine at Mimi Pecci's once more with Rieti (who
tires me) and Marcelle Meyer (about whom, like Germaine
Lubin, they tell atrocities from the Nazi period. But who am I
to enter in? I was not here then). . . Iris Tree didn't say so, but
she was disappointed by the songs to her verse, yet I ask nothing
better than to abandon subtlety and make a fortune. Meanwhile
she is off to Marrakech with the affected and drunken Diana C.
who is Beauty become a urine-hued scarecrow. Well, let them
leave and leave me to my empty problem. This war will hang
and settle us all.

Tomorrow, as Ned Rorem, with Kubly and Bill Weaver I'll

see Naples for the first time, and die perhaps (getting *that* out of the way), and this will pass time. Can I live only hopeless to cry sloppily again in the smell of those caramel triceps. This page, that tree, and love, will soon be long ago.

And I did die too perhaps. I'm back from the hot of the South of Naples which I hated and its beautiful house of opera. There your chain and gold medallion representing *La Madonna del Dito* with the engraved date of our meeting 9-8-54 were stolen by a trapezist (though in my letter I didn't tell you it was a trapezist) and I am maybe punished—though as Bill Weaver said, the chain may one day catch in the trapeze and slit the thief's neck. Punished, I've said, for now returned, Naples, my hemorrhoids have recommenced so viciously that tomorrow I must enter the hospital. Thank you for your letters: how I love you; you are my glass and my key. I long for the fragrance of your arms far off which I see outstretched as we are crucified face to face watching each other die.

No relief. Love means being together; as I am, I grow daily weaker with my Naples illness rejoicing higher always so that I ache and cannot eat nor think of working, going to the dentist. This weekend I will come up to Milano to kiss your feet and beg you to leave and humiliate myself by classic banalities, and you too will turn humble and full of love, and we'll end at the beginning with the insoluable dilemmas. Far from you there's not one friend who doesn't bore me. As I perfect my Italian it becomes the language of my misery. Am sterile and bewitched. The dearest, tedious: Leo Coleman smiles in his Portuguese discs and Petrassi has lent me some rare Gabrieli, but I'm now deaf and blind, and scribbling here has no relief.

Yes, P. came and went and maybe now will come again, and I am going in a week. Back to Paris. After four months in Rome (during which I still haven't finished my *Poets' Requiem* but am covered with new acquaintances, also new wrinkles, paler and older, thinner and smarter, more streaks of peroxide making me red-haired: not really red of course: red hair actually is that usual baby orange of carrots or flame) Mimi Pecci will finally give me a concert next Wednesday in her castle where we'll try out (among other things) Frank O'Hara's *Four Dialogues for Two Voices and Two Pianos* which we'll record next day for the R.A.I. Then I am leaving (all of my new friends and those who've passed by). Back to Paris. By way of Florence and Milan, revisiting old friends and collecting souvenirs. They too'll've grown. Collect too many souvenirs and the basket breaks: that's death. But our baskets are stronger than we think! It's life. . . I'm still in love with you and it will remain so; you, so far from me in every way, loving me, back in Dorno killing a hog each Friday. It won't be long again now. Charley Ford says love means wanting *to live with,* and applies not only to persons but pets and works of art. Back to Paris whose every ash-can is to me a diamond chalice. Our friend Rochas has died in these days, leaving a beautiful wife.

Petrassi thinks that my music—irreproachable though it may be in its traditional frame—lacks the health of adventure.

Before the Evening Meal: I've always liked to do it best before the evening meal. Because thus with a new friend (or old one) we can go out afterwards into the early night's illumination of a strange city (or a familiar one, feeling in love, or out of it) and discuss it all while dining. And drinking; that's making friendships. It used to be that I would drink in order to go to bed; now it's going to bed to be able to drink after and discuss. *Ceci dit* I've slipped only three times since I've come to Rome: once a month is some improvement over once a day. If my hair is sunset-colored . . . if art comes of suffering as they say, perfume too is a monster's infection and sunsets are agitated dirt. Are whales, so good, monsters? Nantucket. Let's go to the islands, any from Nantucket to Lesbos. Real drunks can't sleep. Though I loathe crowds, I love light low closed hotel rooms alone in a huge bed, that magnificent apparatus.

Love before the evening meal in summer (though it could as well be spring when, with the newborn buds, we are moved to wish to utter those same old banalities of love, but to new ears). The first warm days and tinkling carts selling Good Humors in cool suburbs. I find myself whistling the song I made to Edwin Denby's sonnet. Yes, I can whistle and am also somewhat left-handed, can ride a bike "no hansies." (Ride a bike: but in my fantasies of love it is the opposite.)

In America ninety-eight per cent of us are from the "middle class." When Piaf opens her mouth the bourgeois man of France will swoon; she also makes Americans desire a Paris return. *Moi aussi, j'en fais parti.* People wonder: do I love myself or my music more. Is there a difference? I *do* protect myself and with iron ramparts. It's a great love affair! (and before the evening meal).

Florence (the Berchielli): Each cranny and odor I'd forgotten I remember now again in Florence after five years and not a barman's face or restaurant's clientele has changed as though some charm had stopped time with always summer weather here. Left Rome this morning: all was completed there (all except my work in progress), and I am tired, tired. Tomorrow evening P.

joins me; then there'll be Newell Jenkins' concert and tea with David Diamond; the same sight-seeing (that is, the same sights seen with older eyes—but nothing's changed, as though some charm, etc.). Everyone and everything I've seen before I saw once more in Rome which means Judy Garland in her new cinemascope vehicle *A Star is Born* (as long as it is wide) which I admit I saw in Yankton with Janet Gaynor way back when. Today the world's most beautiful woman is surely Elizabeth Taylor. . . Doctor Kinsey still sends his yearly letter to say he's following my career (noted by way of keeping with the times). Rome did nothing much for my vanity (the flesh does grow weary, but alas the most crumpled will still desire: that's the irony). It's no place for drinking: the word *hangover* and its treatment do not exist in Italian: if you have one it's unsafe to venture into the streets: there you risk seeing a decapitated head, a stone dismembered foot, under other circumstances beautiful. Tullio Carminati (who, my age, cannot recall Grace Moore?) flattered me, but what of the old? (when alas the most crumpled, etc.). . . Also I met Lord Montagu in flesh and blood.

Rome: its mediocrity: Favaretto (Italy's Irene Aïtoff). The scandal at the Villa Medici of Jean-Michel Damase (the only talent there) suffering what Edward the Second suffered from the jealous hazing of his fellows, and Ibert shaking his head as though this had not happened. Doda Conrad quotes Nadia Boulanger who says, after a conversation about today's young composers: "Well, after all is said and done, there's really only Ned Rorem!". . .

Part 11
France Again: 1955

Easter's gone.

Sick in bed, throat on fire, a French fever of 38.5. Every year I sink like this because I am a sinner and time grows shorter.

I don't like Paris anymore after these twelve days. I miss whom I love and that's all that counts. It has been months since I have had any impulse to compose and the word *music* causes a pang. I'm awaiting the doctor which is why I write all this. The *poubelles* don't look like grails anymore.

Sick from starting to drink, from thinking I'm the same person in the same place, from a cold and jealousy and boredom and laziness, sick from missing P. who bewitches me ever more tightly after nine months. Probably I'll move completely to Milan.

The doctor came with penicillin, and I'm weary still with throat aflame. Friends too have come and gone, bringing fruit and sandwiches. It's ten in the evening inside, and outside warm spring. I must stay abed and sweat. Friday if I'm well enough I'll go to Hyères two weeks.

❧

Hyères: Einstein died today.

It *is* as always a paradise here. Oscar's a good boy. The Vicomte passed through again (he's a good boy too). The rest of us are correcting proofs: I with the luxury of adding new dedications onto my *Cycle of Holy Songs*; Marie Laure highly nervous about the forthcoming publication of her *Chambre des Écureuils* which seems to be a long-ago dream all the details of which are real but the *whole* becoming a newness from imagination (as in painting, says Nora, where each stroke is trivial while the ensemble is strange).

Poverty's fine at twenty. At thirty, it's unbecoming, being a necessity only to the very young. Today the *avant-garde* is *démodé*. We have other realms to bother us and true adventure no longer glows in the field of arts. I recall first introducing myself to Christopher Lazare by emptying a shaker of martinis over his head at a G.-Village party (he was enchanted). This was a good ten years ago and is the type of gesture I could not repeat today in even my maddest moods. Now we are not concerned with arts, but with jet pilots and atoms. As I grow older the desire for learning, need to read, health of curiosity, leave me increasingly. All answers have been explained and I've understood. But perhaps none of that is true. Why, having learned what there is to know from others, need I now believe in anything but the development of my dreams? I think more of sex than of music. (Should I say: I think more *about* sex than about music?)

In a way I'm still sick from my Paris flu and the everlasting hemorrhoids. But I've begun to soak in sun, and mornings when I pick my ears the wax seems a glittering orange on the nails of my tan hands. I no longer bite my fingernails, by the way—or at least quite seldom.

❧

Couldn't sleep all night because of the strident giggles of Marie Laure and Oscar gamboling on the lawn, drunk, plump, middle-aged, and stark naked. At 4 A.M. Robert Veyron-Lacroix— distressed and bleary-eyed—came to my room for a consultation, and to eavesdrop on this amazing phrase from behind a cypress tree: *"On est vraiment des beaux gosses, n'est-ce pas?"* We decided that if in fifteen minutes they hadn't shut up, we'd douse them from the balcony with a bucket of ice water. Precisely at 4:15 we let the shower descend onto their unsuspecting heads. Then, of course, wide awake, we all laughed together till dawn.

In answer to "Why must painters distort?", ask "What does music mean to you?" People question their eyes, seldom their ears. Is it that since the ear as organ is so much more complex it sifts and chooses on less literal levels? An artist, says Picasso, paints not what he sees but what he thinks about what he sees. Can the same be said of a composer? of a *littérateur*? No. A musician writes what he hears, but *only* what he hears. As for authors, do they notate what they think, or what they think about what they think? No. They write down what they *see*; this holds for both Rimbaud and Daisey Ashford. All creators just see (the composer sees with his ear; mescaline so clearly demonstrates how senses overlap: we witness sounds, hear color, touch tones, taste blues), but since painters see with their eyes they are the most primitive. Gide constructed musically, or so he thought (*Les Faux-Monnayeurs*, if anything, is fugal, and a fugue is formal—rather than rhetorical—only inasmuch as its trademark is contrast of tonalities); in any case he practiced more than, say, Roger Martin du Gard, Aristotle's concept about tragical verisimilitude: "What is plausible and impossible is preferable to what is implausible and possible."

The beautiful are shyer than the ugly, for they move in a world that does not ask for beauty.

Some artists feel superior to this world they live in. But it's *their* world too. Perhaps they depict it better than others, but that very depiction is part of the world.

Eugene List and Carol Glenn are full of good peaches and cereal. They will never go mad.

Why not perfumes with fragrance of fruit as well as flowers? Apple cologne. Pear body-cream. And of course the immortal raspberry. To die in a raspberry. *La mort à la framboise.*

Cannes: It all began wrong. Despite the written invitation from Erlanger I was kicked out of the film festival première because I wasn't in a tux. But I saw the stars' entrances, their congealed smiles, the perfume and flash bulbs and furs, and I swooned a thousand jealousies, and dined alone and did a little walking in the semicold. I want to be a star too like them and have peasants agape at my falseness. Alone in this sexiest of towns I'm a slave to temptations which should never be resisted (our worst memories in old age will be of rejected opportunities), though I nevertheless returned wisely to the hotel (it's only ten-thirty—the Westminster where first I was with Guy six years ago) and will spend the rest of this ruined evening reading the fatuous new Montherlant play, because tomorrow I must rise early to meet P. at the Nice airport. And tomorrow life will take a meaning here where it began. Meanwhile outdoors the back streets are peopled with easy love and I feel voluntarily cheated as in Nuremberg a year ago. Poulenc is here also, and movie folk sufficient to enrapture my wildest associations as in true American inheritance. But it's gratuitously lost for me tonight without

a tux. Oh well! I've the memory of last evening in the hills of
Hyères between the arms of one "whose business has to do with
fish" (as Eliot explained in my sung prayer from "The Dry
Salvages" in '46). Fortunately P. doesn't read English, for the
above is a curious admission from a person to whom fidelity is all.
Really I am *putain*, not in its understanding as *whore*, but in its
French adjectival sense as, say, a dog who, with soulful eyes,
knows how to solicit a lump of sugar, or roll over to get his
stomach rubbed. . . Cannes, darn it! this is a little girl's
entry! My timidity soars as did my snobbery in those poems I
used to write. Heavens, what haven't I done! Piles oppress me.
When I'm thrown out I just leave obediently, tail between legs.
To think that for this I had lugubriously allowed the sun to
scorch me into a raspberry!

Our world's imminent end? Maybe that end came long ago;
maybe we're a race of zombies, the vermin that for millenniums
has clustered with increasing thickness over the earth's corpse.

Stage fright of a martyr: the simple Christian fears the lions
less than his first public appearance.

Plants do not wish to rule the world like us: they have higher
concerns.

Paris: Finished today orchestration of my *Poets' Requiem*.
Fiercely cold, rainy.

Aaron Copland came to lunch today, having read the fifth volume of my journal and we spent the afternoon listening to records of my music. He says the journal expresses the unexpected violent side of my nature, while the music is the less inventive serene side. The music doesn't seem as *necessary* and varied (particularly rhythmically) as with a composer who has *only* this means of speech, especially considering I grew up (I too) in the jazz era. Does my exquisitely laborious manuscript in India ink on transparent ònion skin (a *métier* in itself) represent the most perfect side of my music? Aaron I suppose is the "nice man" *par excellence*, yet my main interest in him is his in me, and if he still intimidates me it's because we first met when I was a child. His worry is that I seem as reconciled to my weaknesses as to my strengths, which indicates I will not change. And growth is change. But he too is a sum of his parts and who's to say where differences and relationships begin in others, let alone ourselves?

Winter's turned to summer in one feathery-yellow day; Paris roads are squeaky-stuffed with baby-buggies. But my nerves feel sawn and knotted: drinking again. Six times since returning on April 13th, six too many, and haven't once made love. Next Saturday I'll take the plane for a few days in Milan, as I can no more stand it alone. Why? when my "career" is abloom in America with fine reviews last week of the opera and symphony, and in a few days the première of *Design* in Louisville, and three concerts in Paris next month? Because I'm bored, weak, shy, lazy, and even the threat of those *lundis cafardeux* does not keep me from wine, with health thinning and fear of work, and the awful post-tender hang-over shaking. . .

Our writers today have lost a sense of words. Could we too say our musicians have lost the sense of notes? We can't now see Rome as an alive place, see a column and say Nero also breathed

on this. Too far ago. Whereas the cave men are just far enough
(like the angel Michael). Sleep after drink is a passion and for
three days it's hard to have enough: we grow like the luxuriant
ruler who enjoyed being awakened for the pleasure of falling
back to sleep. Though *désoeuvré* and guilty-conscienced I'm glad
to be going to Milan, to know that, if the plane doesn't crash, in
five days I'll be in the grip of love without which it is wrong to
live and with which it is also wrong.

Evening with Noël Lee (who is thoroughly good without
being wishy-washy) and played him *The Poets' Requiem*. He
in turn played me his big cantata on Valéry's words which impressed more than any American piece in a long time. Afterwards, having dined rue Mermoz, on his motorcycle we investi-
gated *à deux* the warm Paris roads for three hours, a thing that
should be done alone, and I returned home unelated. The same
happened last night in other quarters with Roditi. If love smiles
bright in the street I'm too coy to capitulate and despise myself
for it.

A month ago with P. at the Cannes Casino I gambled for the
first (probably last) time. The thousand francs we won was spent
on tea and two dishes of raspberry ice cream.

Poulenc was in Cannes, quite recovered from his long illness,
but looking old and smothered in pimples. As he's always been
rather *le cher maître* in my eyes, I was chilled by his talk of
sexual success.

The movie stars in Cannes outraged my life-long veneration,
for they behave like their own caricatures, not as legends. And
they're so old! Movies nevertheless remain my preferred subject
of conversation.

As Philippe Erlanger points out: *les vraies grandes cocottes ne couchent pas*; they are for show.

Italians: How many of them have said to me, knowing me to be Protestant: *"Ah! ma tu non potresti capire, siccome non sei cristiano!".* . . . Their marvelous sense of luxury in disdain of the necessary: the poorest will go without a meal to buy a tie. Luxury (in the sense of a *need* for beauty) is a dying art; it has nothing to do with being rich.

Philippe Erlanger quotes P. in Rome: "Italian duchesses are better than French duchesses because they don't invite me."

Conversation between Mr. G. S. and Mrs. J. B. overheard years ago: G.: "Everything's against me: I'm a Jew, a poet, a Communist, a homosexual, an alcoholic; everything's against me." J.: "That's nothing! I'm Jewish, a poet, a Communist, a homosexual, an alcoholic, and *I'm* a *cripple!*"

Which recalls Djuna's doctor saying: "A broken heart have you! I have falling arches, flying dandruff, a floating kidney, shattered nerves *and* a broken heart!". . .

What is bad cannot endure: it must grow worse.

Before leaving tomorrow again for Milan I'll write a little here to kill time, for I have no more ideas in work, have orgied too much now to orgy more, read all I can, and seen as many movies and friends as are necessary to stay a bit the threat of obliteration.

Ida Rubinstein, who, for years lived next door to Marie Laure here in the Place des Etats-Unis, has (they say) at her ripe age gone as a nurse to a leper colony (just as it's reported that Garbo is to join a nunnery). The Rubinstein house was sold and (to make way for a French six-story *gratte-ciel*) has been reduced to rubble with nothing now left but Diaghilev's dusty recall. We've sniffed about in the ruins of Bakst's blue mosaic garden where Nijinsky died at parties, and Marie Laure, free of charge with her flair for finding the valuable where unexpected, dug from the crumblings twenty superb reproductions of Sebastian (my least-favorite saint: I dislike and am jealous of those who permit themselves to be riddled by soldiers) which were used (caressed) by d'Annunzio and Debussy. It's all gone away now; history is never fabulous as it's being made.

In the *Hommage de la France à Thomas Mann* which came out today (ed. Flinker), I am humble at seeing my name as the only American and one of four composers (with Auric, Milhaud, Honegger) among the seventy-five or so French admirers. Because Mann began my years of "good" reading, until twenty-five when my curiosity ceased.

As Quakers we never used to stand for *The Star-Spangled Banner* (to stand *up* for). Today I realized that this proved little.

An opera libretto cannot be multileveled psychiatry. It must be blood and picnics, hate and drinking-songs, love, ghosts, potions and posies. The music will give it subtlety.

Because I couldn't stand it any longer I went to Milan at the
end of last month to see P. whom I still adore after ten months
of impossibility. We spent a day of heat in Como where one can
no longer sip a pear-juice or nibble a pineapple-sherbet while
moodily thumbing a guidebook *à la* Henry James on a solitary
terrace across from the Duomo. Everywhere today friends must
be met in that only place they come: *la tasse.* But we had love
and cannot consider such things. Anything thrills me in P.'s
presence so the cathedral was a marvel: more appreciable than,
say, the Sistine Chapel which I'd prefer to admire by reproduc-
tion than by craning my neck in the Vatican confines surrounded
by flocks of sweating Swedish female students who've come on
foot from the home country. Claustrophobia's my fever and
liquor my reward.

I went to Milan also because my body wanted love and I don't
know how to look for this in any other way. I have not written
a note in months and feel *désoeuvré,* idealess, filling myself with
aches and gloominess, ridding myself of that by extended going-
out to return with the extenuation of sociability, fall on the bed
and cry, saying: What am I doing here? as, indeed, one could
ask anywhere. Those dreamlike hours which accompany a hangover when carnal obsession attains a peak of daring *et le corps
ne pense qu'à lui-même.* Certain others know this.

Lenny Bernstein has been once more to talk to me of me, and,
though I know no one more astute, I cannot feel close to him
because he *plays* at being close to one, *plays* at being "the real
thing"; his reality's unreal; I like true unreality (hate reality);
Venice is the truth. There is no real difference between the
texture of Scriabine and Berg.

Drink, and recover in order to drink (and recover, in
order. . .). That's how it's been during ever-awful June, and

forever it'll go on, I know. The tension with which I imbibe can
be matched by the delicate care I take to eat liver next day (to
recover—and drink). Meanwhile I don't work, squabble with
laziness, postpone, let time pass.

... *le bonheur d'avoir été malheureux.* [Gaillard on Francis I]

But the memory of past sorrow—is it not present joy?—POE,
"The Colloquy of Monos and Una"

During intermission last week at Ballet Theater I saw Zsa Zsa
Gabor *en chair et en os* (I had met her once with George Sanders
at a party years ago, the first evening of my psychoanalysis). She
is the kind of woman I love (all in yellow, blond, silver, false,
beautiful, shining, affected: the very definition of the Hollywood
Hallucination, the STAR). Well, if I could choose between
remaining a friend of, say, Paul Goodman or becoming one of
Zsa Zsa Gabor's, I'd forsake the former. For Gabor will not last,
and was created to be encountered, smelled, admired. But a great
man is known by his work and is without interest in his private
life. I am a child before the movies.

Aix-en-Provence: Heat.
I despair at twelve-toners: they have lost the need for pleasure.
Music's not written to be understood, but to be *felt*—and grown-
up imaginations cannot perceive it. (Not meant to be understood: yet I am happiest when composing to a vocal text. Is vocal
music an impure form of this most abstract of arts?)
At six we are going to the Casino for the new Boulez work
Le Marteau sans Maître. Boulez has won through intelligence
and personal charm (he looks like Gene Kelly), not because his
music heats hearts. The critics and musicologists, those sterile

ones, are agog before him since finally they can "understand" an emotion explained by words. But where is that necessary union of beauty with the all-important *form* of Nerval, or Piero della Francesca, or Haydn, each filled with the health of inspired bees working toward their hazel-perfect honey?

Hyères: Jean-Louis Barrault and Madeleine Renaud stopped by yesterday on their way back to Paris. They've been preparing their forthcoming production of *L'Orestie* at the nearby nudist colony of l'Ile du Levant. "Communal nakedness, after the first embarrassed hour, is quite antisensual," maintains Barrault. "For stimulation you find yourself saying: 'Get dressed *chérie,* and let's make love!'"

My philosophy was entirely based on the Quaker Church and American cinema.

Drifting back: to earliest high-school summers, midnight swimming, Tom Collins', slow dancing and car radios, learning about sex (which I still haven't learned about), etc. Of course no parent wishes the child to grow up, nor does a child wish his parents to know he has grown up—if he knows it himself, usually too late. My father, in his sixties, tells me he still tells himself: "Tomorrow, when I've grown up. . ." Children just assume their elders know more; what a disappointment to grow up. Because standards stay stationary: I recall my shocked child's tears at old ladies seeking nourishment in ash-cans, but it is no stronger than my grown-up amazement at fellow mediocrity and the laziness of human scavengers. Not that the old ladies were "mediocre"— I had just thought they were like *me.* Poetically speaking, growing up *is* mediocrity.

When I go somewhere today with Marie Laure and Oscar I think people no longer turn to say: *"Voilà la Vicomtesse accompagnée de la Belle et la Bête."* We went to lunch *chez* Christian Dior near Grasse, and he ate hand-in-hand with his Arab acquaintance who's been *rapellé* by the Army. The world's going badly.

Here is the beginning of the end of a season which I seem to have passed without at all writing in this diary; now it's not easy to begin again in a new book, all the more so that I have other problems in progress. But a congenital air for order as well as a fear of chronological loss (like the tourist-monsters incapable of seeing a masterpiece without taking a snapshot of it) make me start here once more. And what have I done in this summer? Contradictions:

Venice. A city where birds live on the ground and lions in the air. . . Venice is a *chef-d'oeuvre* out of context, an isolated masterpiece having nothing to do with Italy, just as *Bolero* can't be included in Ravel's "normal" list of works. Venice is where we quarrel and then make-up, eating grape ice cream on Florian's terrace and watch Chirico stroll by in a yellow sweater as natural as the sunlight. Contradictions of the mid-twentieth century: In Tiziano's portrait Sacred Love is naked and Profane begowned. The *C*'s of Correggio, Carpaccio, Caravaggio once confounded me as did the *M*'s of Maurois and Malraux and Mauriac. Contradictions: Last week was my eighth voyage into Italy where everyone's either rich or poor. In America everybody is *bourgeois,* the poor as well as rich because they live in a place of *bourgeois* habits (just as American Catholics have Protestant natures *because* they inhabit a Protestant country. In France the contrary is true.) In France the friends of Julien Green believe him to be a French citizen; he is not: he's a Catholic convert (to the French it's the same thing).

The worst surprise was discovering grownups had all the weaknesses of children, and none of the strengths.

Marie Laure having gone to meet her mother at a *fête en Arles,* we dined last night in Toulon—Nora, Jacques Février, and Guy de Lesseps whose ancestor, in digging out the Suez which so worries us today, left to his progeny a wit equivalent to the Canal St. Martin. After getting laid (*mon "tapin" quotidien*) in a sordid Toulon room, I joined the others for a good sea-food meal at the Calanque. There is nothing American in this city which entrances me with little lanes, ten thousand sailors, women dining or ironing behind the summery windows at street level. Le Papillon at eleven was jammed with military dancers and intense whores, and a cruel accordionist yelling into a microphone: "Don't forget, *messieurs,* today's Friday, and these ladies have just had their medical; so you won't risk catching clap. Go to it, *les gars,* grab tighter!" My hair stood on end mournfully at these unsmiling faces on the eve of their departure for Egypt.

When I arrive back soon in America (and particularly Chicago: there have been nine years; and I knew each alley, every taste) it will be bizarre as a doll's town frequented by a giant seeking with thick lenses or newborn retinas the old familiar patterns. Less poignant than not recognizing the known, but more alarming, is the reverse phenomenon: recognition of the unknown. Though this occurs for me rarely, it happened again just recently. While in Parma fourteen evenings ago, with P. and Anterro Piletti, we decided to dine in nearby Salsomaggiore. Now I had certainly never seen nor even heard of this bathing village, but the moment I got off the train I knew it all: any signpost, every store-light, each alley or mixture of tastes was familiar, and especially a soaring park seemed more intimate than my pocket. I have known this town only by evening (daylight changes everything); how have I already been here before? in a dream last night? last month? This dismay is familiar to many, intangible and disagreeable.

Later. It has been raining hard for hours; the air and country-side are heavy brown and drenched with ozone, a relief after the continual honey-glitter of the azure coast.

I am exceedingly discouraged about my work. For months my only ideas have been a pallid unspontaneous musical mass of treacle.

Rain, and the room where I write is agrool with a buzz of mating flies who get caught even in my hair and make me shriek. If only this rain could also purify my music, for I don't know into what generation I've been placed. I employ twelve notes designed after a pattern that my own ear craves (all honest com-posers must do this *d'ailleurs*). But am I too young to add new ideas to my elders who are my influence (and who say, "If it were twenty years ago I should follow these children")? Or too old to amuse myself playing with the experimenters who are not precocious but grim? The worst of it is that I just don't care. Meanwhile I read and read, not as an intellectual (I don't seek to instruct myself) but for my realest joy. And meanwhile I play the piano some: the Chopin *Ballades* of my childhood, or old songs of my own making. And meanwhile, it goes on raining.

I have just counted in my Agenda the number of times I have been drunk since the beginning of the year: eighteen! Eighteen times in about thirty-four weeks, or an average of once every twelve days (though in the summer-country I drink once every five weeks, and in winter-Paris twice a week). This is more than I suspected, yet a certain improvement over the years between

1944 and 1952. I haven't drunk two days in a row for over three years; and between drunks when I don't drink, *I don't drink.* Not even wine.

These days, I am no longer interested in filling my address book with grand names, but am turning back instead toward those who've always been solid: relatives, first friends (as for the ego, I would rather, in any case, have the parasites chatter in my small shadow, than to chatter myself in other shadows). Yesterday, despite my continuing difficulty in remaining seated (because, I guess, of a troubled prostate), we drove, Marie Laure and I, to nearby Collobrières to visit the chestnut forest and take tea with *marrons glacés.* As a child, I once screamed to mother, "Look!" as I swung daringly in a tree; but it was not so much the skill of my swing, as the narrowness of the twig I wished her to see. . . P. told me that recently with companions in Dorno he burned a snake alive: at the moment of agony it thrust forth four tiny legs. I was shocked. It was not at the unlikelyhood of a serpent's latent extremities (a serpent already *is* an extremity moving: hence our fear and fascination) as at P.'s childly cruelty.

Maybe I'm too literary for music. When at work on a sizable piece I'm bored before it's a third done: being able to see the bridge's other end eliminates the need for arriving there. I'm too logical. Yet I *réussis* short songs best (they being composed *en un souffle,* in one intake of breath, one "inspiration") which is doubly illogical, song specialists (dealers by definition in poetry) being the least intellectual of musicians.

I am not an intellectual, because I read and reread not to instruct myself but for enjoyment and from curiosity (there!

I *am* curious). I adore discovering origins, seeking comparisons. For instance: Is not *Dorian Gray* a combination of *Roderick Hudson* and *La Peau de Chagrin?* (It's certain Wilde knew Balzac, but could he have read James' book that came many years before his own? James, the only author of quality to straddle the century-point. And who—as Mauriac recently pointed out— troubles us more by what he didn't say than those since Freud who say what *is,* and talk of love in terms of love.) Yes I read and I read and there is never a time when I haven't two or three books under way. But I read junk too. I read more than I compose. I never read what bores me, and cannot read to learn. For we find in books we like only a rewording of what we already knew. Everyone sees the same thing so differently: look in my *Poets' Requiem* at how Gide and Rilke spoke almost simultaneously of animals' liberty; and then I wrote here last May 25th of Nöel Lee's *Cantata* in which Valéry says differently the same words about beasts. It's in the air. But Nöel's notes and mine, as interpretations, have no resemblance (or rather, they *do,* but it's the same difference for the point I'm making). The creatures of Colette, of Butler, are the same, but all sets of eyes converge upon them with separate sympathies. In beauty we discover only what we can understand. The author's name beneath a masterful or mediocre portrait can, alas, adjust our appreciation (Koestler talks of this in his nice but limited essay on snobbery in *Encounter.* Limited, because there's no mention of snobbery's aid to, say, Haydn or Leonardo.)

Mother has just sent a copy of *The Friends' Journal* (a Quaker monthly) in which there's a quotation from *Time* about my opera, saying that Rorem "is, at 32, a master writer for the human voice." First of all I am 31. Second, this opera was composed when I was 26. The public assumes that the date of first performance is the date of creation (not *création,* of course, in the French sense, which means "world première"). Hence, I was a "master writer for the human voice" already at 26 (and, I believe, long before), but this opera is now far behind me and today at 31 (not 32) I'm busy with other interests; it's even possible that when I'm 32 I'll no longer be a master of the human voice. Naturally what I compose today—though perhaps different (if no better)—could not have been done without my experiments (successful or not) of yesterday. Each new work is a result of the preceding one; there is no such thing as a first effort, not even birth. As Gertrude Stein says in a letter to Fitzgerald: "One does not get better but different and older and that is always a pleasure.". . . To return to Wilde by way of parentheses: he (of all people) is represented on the cover of the Quaker journal by the following quotation (undoubtedly intended for future twelve-toners): "He who is in a state of rebellion cannot receive grace, to use the phrase of which the Church is so fond—so rightly fond, I dare say—for in life as in art the mood of rebellion closes up the channels of the soul, and shuts out the airs of heaven."

Are geniuses ever unsure? Because, my God, *I* am!

Julien Green once said that anyone seen with me—man, woman, or child—would automatically be compromised.

Auric, who is doing the music for Clouzot's film on Picasso, brings back this troubling story from Nice. The Master speaks: "The tragic deaths in war are not those of children, but those of the old. A child is quickly replaced (anyone can make one in two minutes) whereas it takes years to make an old man . . ." This is a *bon mot* which, as a pacifist, I don't find amusing.

. . . of all natural forces, vitality is the incommunicable one.
                                          —FITZGERALD, The Crack-Up

Because of my health I haven't been able to work for a week; and while everybody plies me with amiable advice I can just smile and remain in pain. Nora has given me the name of a specialist in Paris where I'm going tomorrow, ruddy as an almond and blond as a peach. Probably I'll get drunk when I arrive and that will settle everything. A summer of witnessing the boozey downfall of others has been instructive, but foreign fire is not our own. I'll learn my lesson when the time comes (as if I hadn't already learned it a thousand times).

What a good little boy I am, back in Paris now and working (songs, and a libretto from Petronious) and seeing all these nice people before whom I lower my eyes, shocked, when Boris Kochno's habits (or somebody else's) are mentioned; but if they knew of the sweat in pure gin that smears my corpse, or my libidinous promenades, their hair would stand on end. Or would it? The truth is I have never really known how to be bad. Sometimes I'm compelled to flee attempts and go south to produce in a disturbed fructuous chastity. For this I can say that, since I've lived in Europe, Marie Laure and Guy Ferrand, in harboring me, have been my closest acquaintances, both in connection with liquor and musical puzzles.

Bright blue smoky clean brisk autumn temperature which every year has that fragrance of trouble and delight that means "back to school" in a bonfire, and I see that shy boy, as through the wrong end of a telescope, growing smaller and smaller in whirling leaves—but for once it's rather pleasant: in less than two weeks I'll be thirty-two.

Marie Laure is still in Hyères (having rightly decided that *Paris sait attendre*) so I'm alone in the great house having breakfast on a platinum tray and sometimes a gold lunch as though I too were rich and noble, and my life is one of movies and

American friends, and I take bouquets of yellow roses to lady friends I haven't seen since spring: Lise, Rina, and Denise *chez qui* yesterday I lunched and had a picture taken by Cecil Beaton. *Voilà.*

Yes, I love to gossip, and I'll narrate the most intimate details of my libido, of a libidinous encounter, to almost any companion (men, not women). But I am discreet, even here in this journal, about what really preoccupies, about concrete problems.

The older we grow the more our first experiences turn sharply etched. The first time I smelled the liquor of a red rose or the honey of a yellow one is clearer today in memory than the seventh time. Problems or joys or terrors or discoveries or hates from ten to twenty now seem in less confusion than from twenty to thirty; and at seven we have so few years upon which to look back that the smallest thrill is all-important, being always the first. But even if I still feel seven, nothing more seems new (though I sometimes *think* so when I'm drunk, while it's only an age-old situation in a reversed scenery at a slightly older—should I say newer?—age), though I suppose *blasé* is life's most insidious adjective. My thoughts feel tarnished; as I said, I'm ill; and, as it's late, I'll go up now to bed.

May I quote myself? "We are only jealous of the young, and we avenge ourselves by falling in love with them. The odor of youth can never be disagreeable."

Poulenc has grown a mustache: his pimples disappear.

The Spanish are dancers; Italians are singers. The Italians have no ear: they *see* their music by substituting themselves for the *prima donna*. Nor can a Spaniard be a spectator; and if he's obliged to sing, feet come clacking out of his throat in a strained *flamenco*. Just as when an Italian dances his feet turn into vocal cords.

It was understood beforehand that during the three-minute wait in Valence I would get off the train a moment to say hello to my friend Jean-Paul Gaël who lives there and was expecting me on the *quai*. Which I did. And before he could open his mouth I began with that timid hilarity which the restraint of time requires me to spout: "*Oh, te voilà! tu es donc venu! Embrasse-moi vite que je te tâte, car les trépidations du wagon ne m'ont fait songer qu'a ça! Et comme je suis nerveux, nerveux! Je sais qu'en te quittant tout à l'heure je me trouverai subitement envahi d'une bizarre tristesse due sans doute à moitié au paysage crépusculaire des environs de Valence* (it was five-thirty in the afternoon), *et à moitié aux cinq minutes impuissantes et fugitives passées ici ensembles sur le quai. Parce que je suis non pas seulement entre deux trains mais également entre deux pays après ces plus de six années françaises. Tu sais que je m'apprête à partir aux Amériques* (I always say it in plural). *Six ans ou cinq minutes, c'est bien une chose fragile que celle des rapports humains vis-à-vis des soi-disantes éternités que l'on passe renfermé en soi-même. Et je me sens ridicule devant ton ami. Ne m'y attendant pas, je n'avais guère préparé mon 'effet' lequel m'est toujours si important.* (He had brought a friend with him *pour éviter la mélancolie,* he later explained in a letter.) *Au revoir.*" And so saying I went back into my compartment leaving him stupefied and mute to watch the train pull out a little while after.

Paris. It appears to blossom at the moment of my going, blossom in fall. *Oh bien sûr, tous les emmerdements habituels*: I have to renew my *carte d'identité*, passport, pack my trunk, see individually six hundred musicians, the numerous details which give me goose flesh. (Jean Rivier, he's the poor man's Florent Schmitt, and that's very poor.) But I'm scared to go, everything stands still, eyes governed by heart see what they're told, and I adore Paris, am scared to go.

The past. New York. Twelve years ago I came wide-eyed into the sin and chic of the Empire City, fresh from Curtis where Menotti was my professor—and professors are above suspicion. Now in those days the specially chic audiences of a particular brand went only to concerts of Povla Frisjh (or Landowska, or later Tourel, or Fizdale and Gold). What was my surprise at seeing Menotti at a Frisjh intermission! These are the contradictions of growing-up. Today Guy Ferrand comes up from the Moroccan nightmare with tales of terrors he was obliged to witness: pregnant women, disemboweled, with small dogs put in the place of embryos; or old women whose vaginas are stuffed with flaming straw. Oh where are we? Oh what I *could* have done. Moravia just wrote about it all in the magazine *Confluence*. I'm so nervous, nervous, nervous, and the tragic liquor of departure. It's Sunday. The nowadays' *entr'actes* will say farewell to me next Wednesday when the Barrault's with Marie Bell give their *L'Orestie* (*musique de Boulez*) which everyone says will be *très long—et très beau*, but nobody says *très beau et très long*.

❦

Our sensitive André Dubois is marrying hard-boiled Carmen Tessier. For years he was a promoter of the "underprivileged," both generally and specifically: he negotiated the Jewish exodus from Germany, and championed Boulez before anyone else did. For years *she*'s been Europe's answer to Louella Parsons with a daily column in *France-Soir*. Though *he*'s now Chief of Police and known as the "Prefect of Silence" (having forbidden honking), *she* continues professionally to be called *La Commère*, or The Gossip. *He*, for years a Gidean admirer of tasteful youth, now says to *her* at parties, "Raise your skirts, *chérie*, and show us the bruises we made last night!" Well, we all evolve; and opposites attract, as Cocteau couldn't help pointing out: *"Le Préfet du Silence épouse la Commère."*

Well, in what country *am* I? Finally I heard the tape of the Louisville Orchestra playing my *Design*. The mechanic of the studio said to me afterwards: "But you aren't of your time." But of course, I *am* of my time, only it is not of me.

La pire chose, c'est de vouloir être à la mode si cette mode ne vous va pas.—FRANCIS POULENC

Rain, drizzle. Rather soft autumn weather. These are my final Paris days (Auric thinks they're the final days of Paris) because in two weeks I'll be on a boat going home. So everything —friends, lawns, neighborhoods, the sky—takes on a deeper, more immediate meaning.

Rubinstein gave a *souper chez lui* last night after his great Chopin concert at the Chaillot and there I found a gorgeous series of former lady-friends who didn't recognize me because now my hair's its normal color. Before them I asked François Valéry (whose dream it is to die in the lions' cage): "A male or female lion?" I guess it's an indiscreet question.

228

Bernard Gavoty, a sad Monday, tells that Honegger spoke of me on his death bed in these words: *"Ned Rorem, lui est vraiment doué avec son goût de la féerie triste. Ce beau nordique, ayant tout, devrait sauter de joie."*

❧

Am I brought back to harness by Robert Phelps's letter? when he reminds me of an unhappy poet once complaining to Colette, who replied: *"Mais personne ne t'a demandé d'être heureux. Travaille!"*

❧

Barring death, there's no old lost forgotten friend we'll never come across again some day. It's a matter of living long enough to learn the size of cycles. But sometimes it would seem better to keep far-ages buried instead of always wishing to find them again, and seeing only wrinkled lovers without conversations. I cannot help the overwhelming memory of snow and poetry in Chicago, at Northwestern, those days, during the learning cycle; the smartest thing I can now do for that lovely sadness, is to keep a thought a thought and not try to remake it squalid-real by stamping back after ten years to find all diminished nut-sized. I knew Roditi when I was a child there; years and years have gone by and now today here we are in Paris which too will be recall. Roditi who recently used these astounding words: "Well, the suffering is over now"; whose little poem of jealousy I've just made into a song, my only valid gesture since returning to Paris twelve days ago, twelve days of tension, all the hysterical nerves of my departure for America without a cent and full of debts: all these big, these little problems cease the day we die. This hovering around the past: I remember in 1936 when as a family we visited Europe; at the American soldiers' cemetery of Belleau Wood I saw mother cry upon the tomb of her young brother buried there long before my birth; I wondered at her tears for something so remote to me; today there is less distance between the first war's end and her tears, than between her tears and the present moment—yet our summer in 1936 is clear as crystal to me. All these are landmarks static in static time; we move from one to another down the road until we reach the one melodramatically signaled with our own end. Then, for all we know, it starts or stops again.

Part 12

Aboard the S.S. United States:
October, 1955

Saw Julien again before leaving and we walked ecstatically through the Palais Royal (where we had been in other weather) into the rue Vivienne (and Julien showed me a house "where wicked things take place—very wicked!" though he wasn't sure on which floor), and on to the little store of the Bibliothèque Nationale to buy a pair of earrings designed as Merovingian owls for his sister Anne, whom he has never allowed me to see.

But none of us is really interesting in what he *does* (even Don Juan, even the headsman) and so an artist invents a marvelous world to which everyone runs with tongue hanging out. I have seen real live princesses; but how old they are, all snobbish and battered. Nobody warned me of this as I read my fairy tales. My tonsils, my hemorrhoids, were torn from my adult body and aged me a decade. Why write of this? I'd rather tell lies.

How many thousands have I spent on perfume and alcohol, cigarettes and Turkish baths, disappointing trips and third-class movies; how many months in silent bars or parks, expecting, in a chair with a book not reading, or waiting in line, waiting in line? Who will tell me it's a loss when I know life must be for pleasure? The parks were balanced by museums, the baths by oceans, bars by composition, and the dreaming chair by books finished. Nothing is waste that makes a memory. Only an American bothers to consider such "justification," turning out souvenirs on the assembly line.

All last night a storm: the boat rolled, stretched, sagged with such energy that I was frightened and envisioned myself on a raft eating my fellows. Today the sun, and we search for whales. I also saw a small blue bird, but none of us knows from where he comes. Toward two this morning I opened the watch Henri gave me before I left, and read again what he had scratched on the metal while a prisoner in Germany: "27-5-40 (and other dates until '42) *Maman, cafard, faim*"; also a flower engraved with infinite patience which, in a prison, would be called boredom (though Maurice Sachs maintained that there one would make love with the whole universe—and, like so many others, he only found real peace in jail). How could I not be moved by these scratched words, I, who was in no direct intercourse with the war and therefore am free to create the wildest inventions, sufficient to flatten out and mute me for life? Yet all around is talk of new conflict as though each rising generation would feel cheated if terror should happen to forget it. Nobody learns, and it is hard to take advice despite five thousand years of fatigue. Must I too die and be replaced?

Is art odd- or even-numbered? The Rockettes are even-numbered ($6 \times 6 = 36$) but the best *corps de ballet* seems odd-numbered—or even-numbered oddly distributed, whereas how can you distribute odd numbers evenly (i.e. in pairs)? Yet iambic pentameter, which would appear the ultimate in odd-numberedness, ends up being in six, since there's an instinctive pause at each line's end. Look at Stravinsky's early odd balance, or Bach's even unbalance. The unexpected (which is art) is always odd, but (as art must) it always evens out. It's as clear in space as in time. One square is a bore (hence the slang: square) while circles are forever magic.

To sleep with a person and be stimulated by images of another. Then to sleep with that other and "succeed" only by images of the first!

In three days we will land in America. I fear a new young electricity after my lazy years. I fear that the streets will be broader or narrower, the days longer or shorter, human smells brighter or duller than I recall. Tricks of memory. Just as our music sounds either better or worse, but never identical to what we heard as we wrote.

On a post card from Elliott Stein in Yugoslavia: *SEE DUBROVNIK AND SPLIT!*

Sober, the business of *daring*: daring to react, be alive; drunk, the avoidance of living, i.e. boredom or breathing. The *courage* for writing music, the obscenity of it! Art means: to dare—and have been right.

Morris Golde tells of the explorer who, age twenty, vanished in Siberia. The widow and young son mourn him long and obsessively. Finally the child, now thirty-five, vows to retrieve his father whom he will recognize by descriptions of clothing last worn. Indeed, after perils and adventures, the corpse is found in ice, a perfectly preserved twenty-year-old with red lips and black hair. The son examines his father now fifteen years younger than himself.

They say women outlive men. They say also that seventy-five per cent of crimes remain unsolved. Now, of these crimes, most are rural poisonings. Is it that wives do not naturally outlive their husbands, but simply kill them off?

Theme for a tragedy. They meet in the morning. By afternoon they are in love. That evening one of them dies.

At the rate of one pack a day for twenty years I've smoked one-fifth of a million cigarettes. And I've passed more time on movies and movie gossip than on music and music copy; my hours of research on Marilyn Monroe alone go beyond those on, say, our lady-authors (I've read them all), not to mention the complete history of music. So life is spent, with crossroads and choices.

Suppose that from the safety of a subway platform you throw a kiss to an unknown paragon in the slowly departing train. But the train *stops!* Its doors reopen, the paragon emerges and approaches you! How much will the knees shake? How will the paragon express unprecedented derision? How will you explain yourself?

Is death an end of illusions? or the ultimate rewarding illusion when we'd thought there'd never be another?

All men are forced into one of two categories: those with eleven fingers and those without.

Oeufs à l'aurore
Gigot de Chevreuil
     Sauce groseille
     Sauce venaison
Purée de marrons
Salade
Endives braisées
Charlotte hongroise
     Sauce chocolat

This was our last lunch at noon, typical of the menu twice a day for four years. Back in 1951 my obstreperousness in the company of Marie Laure was both feigned and short-lived: an expression of dazzlement at so easily meeting half of legendary Europe at her table. Once the novelty wore off, my Quaker sense informed me that, above all, she's offered *the leisure to work*. She has not only provided three pianos, sponsored concerts, clothed and fed and housed me, but has been the main cause of my staying on to compose in France for so long. The glamor of daily life in her mansions of Hyères and Paris—among the richest and yet most "livable" on the Continent—has been balanced by emulating the discipline of her working habits, and by finding the talented child within the spoiled vicountess. (Her unchanneled glee at receiving my gifts of American toilet paper! her French refusal to stop a conversation even while on the *bidet!* her suave ignorance of my midnight strangers in her purple sheets! her tolerance of cripples!) She has been my chief *confidante* and adviser; as sheer instruction goes, she corresponds in the French fifties to what Virgil Thomson was for my American forties. My parents excepted, there is no doubt that she and

Virgil are the two "older" people who've most influenced my thinking and my style.

If I could live hidden as a hermit I should be utterly happy, but having been born for notoriety my nature will remain obstinately sad. Nevertheless the moment of making is at once the loneliest and happiest one can have. It is the time between these timeless outbursts which excruciates, as it's then we're lost. What difference if our art has been spoken before: every new generation demands in living words the same morals, horrors, same ecstasies, which have already been as frequently reproduced as the number of seasonal rebirths since earth began. There is no evolution, we never learn; we merely change language and styles every decade or so. The marvelous clamor of science has aided in little things, lengthened our life, but has never made us good. Is it any wonder my father has signed up to go to Mars?

When idiots on boats say, "Where do your ideas *come* from?" I answer that it can't be explained. When clever laymen ask, I discuss the process at length. But when other artists talk of this, I say, "Ideas? I *steal* them." And they understand. Sometimes I rob myself.

The entire ship's been interlaced with a series of temporary ropes, as complex as the thongs in a spider's web, which we must clutch, as more bad weather's expected.

A diary has impact only through the accumulation of un-limited observations (of which many are obsessive and recurring), never through the development of themes (for then it would no longer be a diary). Works of art must have a plan; beginnings and ends. A diary necessarily has no form beyond the accidental one of improvisation; hence, though it cannot be a work of art (improvisation precludes this), perhaps it *can* be a masterpiece.

The fact of writing here turns an experience into an idea. If I were to keep a diary instead of a journal, I would ultimately forget having lived, would remember only what I'd written about having lived. Man's horror is language: Chaos and Order are mere inventions. If, ten billion years back, one cell had slipped a fraction, how different today would be our concept of things.

John Ashberry says: "Once you've been happy in Paris you can never be happy anywhere else—not even in Paris."

Alas, I am happy! Despite complaints or broken hearts (my several hearts); despite this sometimes mournful book that demonstrates less the need to explain than to document myself; despite the hangovers which, like mescaline, make me a vegetarian; or that hardly a day begins without my wondering if I'll die before dusk; despite the schmaltz of eternal youth—I eat with good appetite, sleep and screw well when not working well, and am, as they say, *appreciated*. And so, though the style was always tragic, larger than life, today I'm happy, alas! (happiness, for me, being contained almost exclusively in routine and good weather).

The day after humanity dies there will still be huge atmospheric storms in midocean as there were ten thousand years ago, but nobody left to imagine them.

Yesterday was my birthday. Tomorrow we arrive in New York. Already it appears to have happened to another child. Who knows if America might not after all be the country where my *realest* problems, for better or worse, will eventually be solved?

I asked her if I would find love again back home.
But Marie Laure replied: *Quant à moi, je n'ai plus envie de faire l'amour, je veux faire l'amitié.*